HOPE
In The Darkness

Stories of Rescue and Redemption

SAJI LUKOS

Written By

GRACE BENSON

Mall Publishing Co.

THE PRINTED WORD THE PLANTED SEED

What others are saying about Hope in the Darkness

"As Americans we can be so out of touch with the harsh realities faced by the children in India. This book beautifully chronicles the stories of some of those children and the way that God has used Dr. Lukos and his ministry to be Jesus' hand extended."

— Rabbi Michael LaPoff,
Congregation Beth Sar Shalom, Tucson, AZ

"I have been blessed to actually walk the streets of India with Saji Lukos. There is no one better equipped than Saji to bring attention to the gut-wrenching plight of India's children. On the other hand, there is no one better to bring forth biblical solutions so that more of these children can live up to their full potential."

— Kevin James, *Pastor*

"This book puts names and faces to the difficulties faced by many children in India through stories that are both heartbreaking and heartwarming. Perhaps even more importantly, it will enlarge your vision of the heart of a gracious God who persistently brings hope to the hopeless."

— Will Spink

"Looking at the world around us can be discouraging as we see the direction our culture and Country are going. However, as believers in Jesus Christ we are called to be the salt and light to a lost world trapped in darkness. Hope In The Darkness is a fantastic collection of powerful true stories that will encourage your heart and stir your soul as you see the power of God rescuing little lives who were lost."

— Chad Christiansen,
Founder of In The Gap, Oklahoma City, OK

Dedicated to all

the Mercy Home children and

those who minister to them

Grace Benson with children of The Nagpur Mercy Home.
There are Mercy Homes in several states of India.

In front of The Nagpur Mercy Home

Introduction

After I preached on Saturday at Congregation Beth Sar Shalom in Tucson, Arizona, I was talking with people at the RIMI display booth. A handsome young boy, Paul LaPoff, son of my good friends Michael and Nancy LaPoff, interrupted the conversation, looked into my eyes and asked, "Mr. Lukos, do you have something for me to read from India?" I was deeply moved and inspired by his moving question; I responded to him, "Yes, Paul, you will have something to read soon. This experience truly inspired and motivated me to share the stories of our children in India among whom we are making a huge difference with the love of Jesus Christ.

Grace Benson was my answer from God. Grace's father and I studied at Trinity International University almost twenty-five years ago. I knew Grace when she was just a young girl. She was growing in the Lord with a heart for God and passion for missions. She was bright and talented. Grace volunteered for a ministry called "In The Gap" where she enjoyed tutoring and teaching children for two years. That experience confirmed her desire to serve children. Later, she was invited to go to south India on a short-term mission trip where she taught at two different schools. As the years past, her heart for children and India continued to grow. She got really connected with the children of India. I asked Grace to consider going to Nagpur and interview many of our children whom we love and take care of in our Mercy Homes. She was so kind and gracious to accept the challenge and went there. She touched the lives of our children with her love and compassion. She enthusiastically interviewed them and collected their stories to share with the children of America and beyond. I am grateful to Grace for writing and editing these stories. Thank you, Grace! My God is faithful to reward you for your labor.

Why do we need to tell their stories? God created all children in the image of God, and thus each person is so unique, precious and made for His purposes. Unfortunately, this truth is not taught everywhere. Children are at risk. We must be a voice to the voiceless. Around 1.2 million children died of preventable causes in 2015 in India before their fifth birthday (UNICEF). This is unacceptable. At a hospital in West Bengal, 35 children died within five days due to lack of proper care.

Many children are sacrificed to gods because of ignorance. Injustice is done to children everywhere. A mother offered her child in the Ganges River for the forgiveness of her sin and guilt. A man in South India sacrificed his child to goddess Kali seeking "diving powers". We must "untie" them and rescue them so God can fulfill His purposes in their lives

RIMI has a bold vision to deliver children from poverty and injustice. We have a God-sized dream to help 25,000 children through various child development programs. Every day, children's lives are being transformed by the love of God and compassion of His people. Many of our children are changing lives in many parts of the world. Just to name a few, Raja works in Dubai, Lala serves as our accountant and Komal is preparing to be a nurse. They are transformational leaders are making a huge differences wherever God is placing them. That is why we are passionate to share their stories. We want parents to share these heart-touching stories with your children so that their children will be grateful for what they have and develop genuine compassion for the poor children of the world, especially those in India." Unfortunately, by the influences of this world, we are becoming more and more selfish and individualistic. This is dangerous.

I am confident that these true stories of children will move the hearts of millions of people worldwide for Christ's glory. It is my prayer that as you read this book, you would ask the Holy Spirit what you can do to rescue the suffering children of India and beyond from poverty and injustice. Apostle James says that, *"Religion that is pure and undefiled before God, the Father, is this: to visit orphans and widows in their affliction, and to keep oneself unstained from the world."* We must act now in obedience to God, if we are truly His children.

– Saji K. Lukos

Acknowledgment

Praise the Lord for all the people who gave their time, testimonies, prayers, and resources for this book. I am very grateful to all the children in India who shared their stories with me. The apostle John wrote, *"And there are also many other things which Jesus did, which if they were written in detail, I suppose that even the world itself would not contain the books that would be written."* (John 21:25). In the same way, there are so many stories about what God has done and so many children's lives the Lord has transformed, that if I tried to write about every answered prayer, it would take a lifetime. Although all their stories are not in this book, I saw in each child's life a picture of Christ's indescribable love.

I would like to thank all the staff at Mission India Theological Seminary who cared for me, took time to drive me, and helped me in various ways. I am also grateful for Molly "Auntie" John for giving me advice and helping me at the Mercy Home. Sarita Samuel, Rinki Tembhurne, and Jayshila Nandeshwar went the extra mile in showing love to me. I am so grateful for their friendship, hospitality, and prayers. Their passion for Jesus and willingness to do whatever He asks regardless of how hard it may be is humbling. Similarly, Pooja Chinnappa, Nikita Sable, and Lalita Londhe sacrificed their personal time to translate for me during interviews. Without their patience and perseverance, I would not have been able to finish this project.

I would also like to thank my family and friends from around the country who prayed for me and encouraged me to complete this book. The people in my small group from Cornerstone Fellowship Bible Church and leaders from In the Gap ministry were a tremendous encouragement and support. I would like to give a special thanks to Elisa Joulfaian for her faithful prayers. She encouraged me to step forward in faith with this project and continued to send me prayers and encouragement both while I was in India and after I returned to the states. I would also like to thank all those who edited this book. My mother, Sarah Benson, and my friend, Melanie Corse, spent hours editing, praying, and encouraging me.

I am grateful for Saji Lukos and his vision for ministry to India. It is an honor and privilege to write this book in support of what God is doing in His kingdom. It is my prayer and belief that God will use this book to bring glory to Himself and to touch the hearts and lives of those who read it. I am humbled that God choose to allow me to see glimpses of His heart for the children and the lost of India. As Psalm 126:2-3 says, *"Then our mouth was filled with laughter and our tongue with joyful shouting; then they said among the nations, 'The Lord has done great things for them.' The Lord has done great things for us; we are glad."* I want to declare God's greatness so that all who hear will praise the Lord.

Table of Contents

Chapter 1 - Another Father 1

Chapter 2 - Stolen 7

Chapter 3 - Precious Oil. 13

Chapter 4 - Forsaken, but Not Forgotten 17

Chapter 5 - They are Weak, but He is Strong 21

Chapter 6 - You have the Answer. 25

Chapter 7 - Unwanted 29

Chapter 8 - Worth Saving. 33

Chapter 9 - From Confusion to Comfort 39

Chapter 10 - Respect and Responsibility. 43

Chapter 11 - He Will Carry Me .47

Chapter 12 - A Plate of Food 51

Chapter 13 - I Want to Go Home. 55

Chapter 14 - Without Him, I am Nothing 61

Chapter 15 - Shielded. 67

Chapter 16 - A Miracle in Me 71

Mercy Home boys eating a nutritious meal

CHAPTER 1

Another Father

"Safety does not exclude suffering. I learned that to trust in the strong arms of Christ means that even our suffering is under control. We are not doomed to meaninglessness. A loving purpose is behind it all, a great tenderness even in the fierceness."
— *Elisabeth Elliot, Missionary to Ecuador*

She halted when he rode past her on his bicycle. She didn't know the boy, but the sight of the bicycle sent pangs of agony and longing through her. Her father and his bicycle were gone, it was useless to wish him back, but it hurt to be reminded of him. It hurt so much. A single tear fell on the ground. Her lips quivered, but she stubbornly pressed them closed and sucked in her breath like she watched her older sister do. Somehow, the seven year old found the strength to restrain her grief. Sakshi (pronounced "sock-she") straddled the ditch, staring at the ground. Her plastic flip flops were ripped at the heel, but they were the only shoes she owned. She had to be careful not to step on glass or sharp rocks in the ditch. The murky brown water flowed between her feet as if mocking her with its speed and agility. Frustrated, Sakshi kicked the water, but it didn't make her feel better. Just then, she heard her older sister's voice. She beckoned her inside, reminding her to sweep the floor before their mother came home.

Sakshi trudged inside the room, thankful that she only had one room to clean. Picking up the straw broom, she dutifully started sweeping. Her mother cleaned other houses to earn money. Some of the houses her mother swept were made of tin and others had real glass windows. Staring back at the street, Sakshi wished that her house had real windows. They could not afford them, so they had a single hole in their mud wall which served as a window.

When her mother returned, Sakshi thrust the broom in the corner and hugged the frail young woman. Reverently, the woman bowed towards the miniature figures of Laxmi ("lock-shmee") and Ganapathi ("gone-a-pot-tea") on the floor in the corner of the room. Although Sakshi's mother took her and her sister to the temples only on holidays, they were still careful to honor the Hindu deities when they could. Her mother nodded approvingly at the clean floor, and then urged Sakshi to play outside.

Obediently, Sakshi returned to the street, dodging the motorcycles and cars. It was dusk, and the gray sky seemed to match her mood. Shivering slightly, she wished she had a chuni ("choo-nee"), or scarf to keep her warm. As her sister reminded her, scarves were a luxury. She was lucky enough to know the location of an abandoned shed where she could use the bathroom in privacy. Most people in her caste had to go in the ditch. Sakshi detested the ditch and wondered why the government would not install proper pipes. Perhaps pipes would not do very much, since no one in her slum could afford a bathroom with a roof. Rounding the corner Sakshi bumped into a tall man. He caught her hand to keep her from falling backwards into the ditch.

"I'm sorry; child, are you alright?" the man asked courteously. Startled, she pulled away. She wanted to run back home, but his smile fascinated her. She couldn't remember the last time a man had smiled at her.

"You look cold. Here, please take this; my wife sent it with me in case I needed it." He pulled a dark yellow scarf out of his backpack and wrapped it around Sakshi's shoulders. Speechless, Sakshi gaped at him and gathered the scarf tighter around her thin body.

"What is your name, and where do you live, child? Is your family home?" His tender voice warmed her heart.

"My name is Sakshi…my mother…" she stammered. Taking her hand in his, the gentleman motioned for her to lead the way.

When they arrived at Sakshi's house, the gentleman waited while Sakshi went inside. In Indian culture, it is not acceptable for a man without his wife accompanying him to enter another man's house. At the sight of the dark yellow scarf, Sakshi's mother jumped back in alarm. Her sister gasped when she saw the man's shadow in the doorway and clung to her mother's dress. Sakshi explained that a kind man loaned her the scarf and he wanted to see them. Bravely, Sakshi's mother came outside to meet him. He introduced himself as Santosh (pronounced "sawn-toe-sh") and reassured her that he was just a neighbor stopping by to introduce himself. She offered him tea, but he politely declined, saying that his wife had dinner waiting for him. Sakshi couldn't stop staring at him. Santosh's clothes were simple and his manner was soft and genuine. He promised to bring his wife Sita (pronounced "sheet-uh") to visit them the next day.

While her mother and sister slept beside her, Sakshi squirmed with anticipation. Would Santosh really return? Why was he being so kind? She imagined Sita and how gentle she would be. Were they trying to gain their trust in order to exploit them? In a few hours, the sun came up and Sakshi's mother left for work. Sakshi and her sister could not go to school because they did not have the money to pay for admission fees. Instead, they spent their time wandering around the city and cleaning their tiny home. All afternoon, Sakshi ran back and forth, scanning the streets for the man and his wife.

After Sakshi's mother returned home from work, Santosh and Sita came to visit them. The adults talked for a couple hours, and Sakshi memorized the loving expression on Santosh's face. They learned what happened to Sakshi's father, and how he used to hire himself as a bicycle rickshaw driver, but he was an alcoholic. Two years ago, he never came home. His family learned about his death several days later. Sakshi shrank into the corner when her mother mentioned her father. The tears coursed down her cheeks. Her sister pinched her for being disrespectful to their guests by crying, but to their surprise, Sita reached over and touched Sakshi's chin. Tenderly, she reassured Sakshi that she was not offended and Sakshi did nothing wrong by crying. She knew what it felt like to lose a loved one. Santosh explained that he and his wife are Christians. They purchased an apartment nearby specifically so that they would have a place to teach children who live in the slums and cannot afford to go to school. They invited children to their home in three shifts in order to serve 200 children each day. Santosh and Sita offered to tutor Sakshi and her sister for two hours at their apartment. If the girls had permission to come, then they would be able to learn reading, writing, math, morals, songs, games, and personal hygiene for six days each week. Sakshi's mother gratefully accepted their

offer. At the end of the visit, the couple brought Sakshi's family to the apartment so that the girls would know where to go the next day, and everything was settled.

The following afternoon, Sakshi and her sister arrived at Santosh's house. Many other children were coming from all directions, happily climbing the five flights of stairs, lining up their shoes in an orderly fashion, and filling the apartment with friendly chatter. Inside the apartment, the young pupils sat on the floor in the main room and adjacent kitchen facing Santosh's desk. First they listened eagerly to Santosh's lesson, and then they sat quietly and raised their hands for Santosh and Sita, respectfully obeying and basking in their encouraging smiles. Sakshi could hardly believe that she was going to start learning.

As the days and months turned to years, Sakshi learned how to read and write in Marathi (the state language of Maharashtra), Hindi, and English. She made friends with several other girls from her slum who were also Santosh's students. Sita also tutored her and was always available if Sakshi needed advice or someone to comfort her. When Sakshi first started coming to Santosh and Sita's house, she was extremely shy and timid. She didn't want to answer questions in front of everyone, and she often cried about her father. Both Sita and Santosh spent time helping her with her studies and talking to her about her father. Through their sacrificial service, Sakshi observed true leadership. She realized that education unlocks the door to opportunity, and those who are educated are responsible to help the people around them.

Sakshi quickly became a leader among her peers, volunteering to answer questions and even help the younger students with their homework. Although she is only twelve years old now, she is bold, confident, and hopeful. Sakshi's dream is to become a collector for the IAS (Indian Administrative System) so that she can help bring change to the system of corruption and help the poor people in her community. Collectors are the heads of their counties, and they make executive decisions similar to those of mayors in the United States.

According to Sakshi, she is no longer without a father. "My father's name is Santosh. He counseled me after my father's death. Before, I was unable to see a bicycle without missing my father, but now, I am a leader. Someday, I will make a difference in my county just like Santosh Sir is doing today." Pray that Sakshi will come to know her heavenly Father and rest in His love above the love of all others.

Psalm 68:5-6 - "A father of the fatherless and a judge for the widows is God in His holy habitation. God makes a home for the lonely; He leads out the prisoners into prosperity, only the rebellious dwell in a parched land."

God sends His children to show others what He is like. He is a perfect Father and does not leave His children alone or unprotected. When you feel lonely or afraid, think about Jesus. Ask Him to send people to you who will help you to understand how much He loves you. Pray for the orphans in India and around the world today. Pray that they will come to know Jesus and that God will bless and lead the Christians who are serving them.

Santosh and Sita who work with Mission India use their home for CDC (Child Development Center) – Santosh is pictured standing on the left

CHAPTER 2

Stolen

"You can give without loving, but you cannot love without giving."
— *Amy Carmichael, Missionary to India*

Preatik (pronounced "pre-teak") wondered how long he had left to live and what was in his future. Although he was only nine years old, the doctor had warned that he could die if he did not get a special operation to remove the boils on his body. The operation cost 5,000 rupees, which is about seventy-three dollars, an amount that Preatik's family could only dream of seeing all at once in their lifetime. They lived in a stick hut in a slum near the city of Nagpur. His parents were from a low caste, which meant that the only type of work they were allowed to do was to collect garbage and sweep the streets of richer families in their area. His mother tried to save some money for Preatik, but his father usually found it and spent it on alcohol.

One afternoon, Preatik and his older sister Achal (pronounced "ah-chall") heard a Christian man named Santosh (pronounced "sawn-toesh") telling stories in their slum. The children were invited to start going to school at Santosh's apartment which was nearby. They eagerly accepted and started attending regularly. Preatik's parents did not have much time to take care of their children because they were very poor and had to work all day long in order to buy food.

"Are you finished cooking the rice?" A gruff voice broke the stillness of the room as Preatik's father stood in the doorway. Preatik's mother, who had come home earlier to prepare food for her husband, lowered her eyes and nodded. She noticed the growing puddles of rainwater around her and looked up at the thin roof. Sadly, the orange plastic cover that her husband salvaged from the trash was not waterproof. Preatik's father sat down on the ground and waited while she served him a plate of rice and some watery curry. Respectfully, she stood nearby while her husband ate. In Indian culture, the wife will not eat until her husband has eaten. As she watched his large hands, she wished that he didn't have to clear garbage off the streets. Chiding herself for wishing for something that she thought the Hindu gods did not give her, she decided to ask her husband about Preatik.

"How can we help Preatik? I am worried about what will happen if he does not get that operation the doctor told us about." Her soft tone betrayed her fear.

"I told you, the boy is fine. Those boils will heal in time. Besides, you know what I think about education. Achal and Preatik don't need to be educated any more than you and I do. They are our children, so they will become garbage collectors like us. As long as you send them to that apartment school, you're just filling their heads with western ideas. It's useless." He pushed his plate towards his wife and rose to leave. Silently, she picked up the plate and gazed at him pleadingly. Ignoring her, the man stalked out into the rain. Crestfallen, she sensed that he would not want to clean streets in the bad weather. She wondered if he was going to get a drink and when he would return home.

Preatik brushed past his father on his way inside the house. He had just returned from his daily errand to the market. Poor families in India send their children to buy food every day because they do not have enough money to buy more than a few meals at a time. Preatik's thick hair was dripping wet and his stained clothes were dotted with holes. Smiling brightly, he handed the groceries to his mother and gave her a hug. Wearily, she thanked him and sat down on the dirt floor. Preatik rinsed his hands in the clay water basin and sat next to his mother. He was careful to turn his face away from her as he sat down so that she wouldn't see him wince in pain.

"Son, you're nine years old today." She tried to sound cheerful as she touched his cheek. Standing up, she went to get two plates and returned with their simple meal. The two ate silently, each wondering what the other person was thinking.

"Do you think I'm old enough to work yet, mother? I want to help you earn the rest of the money the doctor asked for. Someday when I'm well, I'll pay you back." His mother did not want to tell him that the situation was worse than he thought. Preatik rinsed his plate and hands in the clay wash basin and went into the corner of the hut to collect his backpack.

Waving goodbye to his mother, Preatik ducked outside. The rain fell in sheets, washing the filth from the huts and sending waste coursing through the ditches. Gingerly, Preatik picked his way through the puddles and potholes. He wished he could run, but he was afraid to try because the boils might spread and grow even more. It was hard enough to climb the five flights of stairs to his teacher's apartment.

"Good afternoon, Preatik!" his teacher's wife Sita (pronounced "sheet-uh") greeted him. "How is your mother? You must be cold, you're soaking wet." Preatik nodded and placed his sandals on one of the stair steps with the other fifty pairs of shoes. He saw his older sister Achal's shoes already there. She must have come straight from the house where she had been cleaning garbage that morning.

Picking his way through the other students, Preatik found his place near the left wall. His favorite subject was writing, and he dreamed of becoming an engineer. He also enjoyed the art lessons that Sita gave the students. Sita saw Preatik wince as he sat down and shook her head. As the child opened his backpack and pulled out his notebook, Sita resolved to visit his mother the next day.

The following morning, Sita stopped by Preatik's house on her way back from the market. "I wanted to ask you how Preatik is feeling and if you have managed to collect the rupees for his operation yet."

His mother buried her face in her hands. "He tries to be strong for me, but I can tell that he is in pain. I am afraid that he is getting worse." She paused to wipe her eyes, then continued, "My husband left yesterday afternoon and hasn't returned. He must have found the scarf where I hid the money I was saving for the operation. What will happen to Preatik?" She sobbed.

"Only Jesus Christ can help you. You must pray to Him. He is the only true God." Sita said comfortingly.

Preatik entered the house and stopped in surprise. He didn't expect to see Sita visiting his mother. When he realized that his mother was crying, he guessed what had happened.

"Has the money been stolen again, mother? Where is father?" he asked anxiously.

Her tear stained face confirmed his guess. "If there is a god, only he can help us." Preatik concluded.

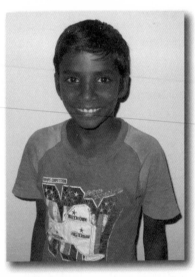

Sita raised her head and turned to her student. "There is." Her steady, peaceful gaze warmed him inside, but Preatik couldn't understand why. "His Name is Jesus Christ, and He alone can heal you."

Preatik thought about what Sita said about Jesus. Would Jesus be able to heal all his boils? Could he stop his father's drinking habit? Could he give his mother enough money to not worry anymore? Could He give Preatik an engineering degree? Preatik wanted to believe that there was a God who had the power to change his life. Looking down at his soiled clothes, he resolved not to become a garbage collector and to find out more about this Jesus.

Standing up, Sita reached into her pocket and handed Preatik everything she had. Preatik counted twelve rupees, which is equal to approximately eighteen cents. He could buy salt for two rupees, oil for five rupees and rice for the next day. Even though Sita and her husband did not have very much money, they generously shared whatever they had with their neighbors. Gratefully, Preatik hugged Sita. He had begun to believe that his future was not stolen. He had begun to believe that Jesus would heal him. He had begun to believe.

Proverbs 11:25 & 30 "The generous man will be prosperous, and he who waters will himself be watered. The fruit of the righteous is a tree of life, and he who is wise wins souls".

The wise man trusts God to give him what he needs and generously shares what God has given him with others. You can share what God has given you with others too. Being generous doesn't always mean you have to share or give money to others. It can be as simple as sharing the joy that Jesus gives you by smiling at a stranger, using your strength to help your parents, or telling your friend about Jesus. Maybe you can share something with someone who is not a Christian, and God will use your generosity to help that person learn about Jesus. When you are generous, you are showing the world who Jesus is.

Children ready for school

Santosh and Sita's school

Washing pots during daily chore time

CHAPTER 3

Precious Oil

"God is in control, and therefore in everything I can give thanks, not because of the situation but because of the One who directs and rules over it."
– Kay Arthur, Author and Bible Teacher

The oil glistened in the firelight. Mahatu (pronounced "ma-ha-too") slept peacefully, oblivious to the fact that his wife and daughter were praying for him in the name of Jesus. Ruchita's (pronounced "roo-cheat-uh") uncle and older brother slept on the mat beside him. Since her father would never permit them to pray over him if he was awake, Ruchita and her mother waited until he slept to lift him up before the Lord. Carefully, Ruchita's mother poured the fragrant oil on her hand and rubbed it on her husband's scalp ever so gently so that he would not stir. The lady who gave them the oil encouraged them to use it when they prayed as a reminder that their prayers were a fragrant aroma to the Lord. As she knelt beside her mother in prayer, Ruchita remembered the time that she and her mother had visited a Christian church service. It was beautiful, and the pastor even had his own Bible, something that is rare in their area. If only Mahatu hadn't forbidden them to attend, Ruchita would have walked there every Sunday.

After they finished praying, Ruchita and her mother lay down on the floor a few paces away from the men and kissed each other goodnight. Turning on her side, Ruchita scanned her home contentedly. The mud hut was not attractive in any way, but to her, the metal roof seemed good enough to be in a respectable neighborhood. In heaven, everyone will live in a beautiful house because God is good, just like He is while we are here on earth, she mused. Ruchita breathed a prayer of thanks to Jesus for giving her a safe place to sleep every night and a mother who loved and prayed for her. She fell asleep dreaming about heaven and all that God had given to her.

Before the sun rose, Ruchita and her family started preparing for work. Mother bustled around cooking rice and gathering her cleaning utensils for her job as a maid. The men tied coils of rope around their waists to help them secure the abandoned pieces of furniture they hoped to salvage that day. They worked for a man who took things that had been discarded in rich neighborhoods and re-designed them in his shop. They sold the recycled furniture for low prices to middle class people and split the money. Sometimes the work was plentiful and other times they did not find anything to re-design. When the men at the shop do not have work, they usually buy alcohol and drink together. Sometimes Ruchita accompanied her mother to other homes to help her cook and clean, but today, her job was to take care of their home.

Waving goodbye to her family members, the industrious thirteen year old picked up the two five gallon buckets and went to fetch water. If she didn't fill the buckets all the way, she could use her left hand to balance one on her head, and her right hand to carry the second one. Thankfully, the family who shared their tap water with Ruchita's family only lived a few narrow streets away. Carrying water wasn't a chore to Ruchita, it was a daily adventure. She viewed each day as a gift from God with many opportunities to talk to Him. Half an hour later, Ruchita came home with the buckets of water. She sat down to rest for a few minutes, then poured some of the water into a small basin and started washing the rice pot. The little bar of turquoise soap had lasted them several weeks thanks to her mother's frugality.

As she worked, Ruchita thought about God's cleansing work in her family. Four years ago, Pastor Santosh (pronounced "sawn-toe-sh") and his wife Sita (pronounced "sheet-uh") came to Ruchita's home. They shared the gospel with everyone except her father, who was out drinking. Her brother and uncle left scoffing, but Ruchita and her mother recognized their need for forgiveness and accepted Christ as their Savior. Santosh and Sita offered to educate Ruchita at their apartment every evening. Ruchita was thrilled to start studying, but her favorite part of the day was prayer time with her mother. The two would pretend to sleep, then get up and kneel together to pray. For two years, they prayed that Mahatu would stop drinking, and he did. He claimed that he had completely lost his taste for alcohol.

Ruchita started to sweep the floor. Several wilted flowers lay scattered around the room. They had fallen from the pictures of the Hindu gods that the men worshipped. The Lord was working on her father's heart. Ruchita hoped that someday he would realize that those items were nothing more than pictures.

"Lord," Ruchita prayed, "thank you for giving me the truth. I believe that Jesus Christ died to pay the price that I could never pay. I know that you are the only true God. You love children, and you love me. I want to know you more, Jesus. Thank you for my Christian teachers Santosh and Sita and their love for you. Thank you for my friends who are studying with me under Santosh Sir. If you want me to be a doctor, help me to study hard and learn what I need to know. Even though I can't go to school, you gave me a school in Santosh and Sita's apartment. Jesus, someday, I want to have my own Bible. I want to be able to read it to my whole family. Please help the Christians who have Bibles to share with the people who don't have them. Only you know how much I want a Bible, and only you can send one to me. You have given so much to me. I will thank you as long as I live. Amen."

Pushing the pile of dirt out the front door, Ruchita remembered something Sita had told her. The Bible says that when families and neighbors live together peacefully and without arguing, it delights the Lord, just like the fragrant oil. Ruchita imagined her family gathered around reading the Bible together. As far as she was able, she resolved to live a life that is pleasing the Lord, just like the precious oil.

Psalm 133:1-2 - "Behold, how good and how pleasant it is for brothers to dwell together in unity! It is like the precious oil upon the head, coming down upon the beard, even Aaron's beard, coming down upon the edge of his robes."

Only God can give us the grace to have peace and dwell together in unity. You can practice being a peacemaker in your family by talking and listening to others. God will help you learn to put others before yourself and forgive those who hurt you. You can also pray for unity in your family and for Christians all over the world.

Mercy Home children playing a game during free time

CHAPTER 4

Forsaken But Not Forgotten

"God's work, done in God's way, will never lack God's provision."
— Hudson Taylor, Missionary to China

Wincing, he opened his eyes. The ceiling looked as bleak as he felt inside. He pressed his hands over his ears in a feeble attempt to block out the chaos. His parents were fighting again. With a sigh, he squeezed his eyes shut and willed himself back to sleep. Rupesh (pronounced "roo-pesh") lived with the constant sound of his parents fighting. Any time they were together, it seemed as though they were at war. At least the house was quiet during the day when his father was working at the factory. Rupesh watched his mother cook rice for him to eat while he sat on the floor. He had no siblings to play with him, and he was left alone hour after hour. He wondered if anything would ever change.

Instead of their usual routine, Rupesh and his parents walked towards some unknown place for what seemed like hours. Rupesh closed his dry lips and longed for water. Finally, his father pointed to a small building in the distance. His mother glanced up, and then lowered her head again. Rupesh wondered what they were thinking as they continued to shuffle along the dusty path towards the city of Wadi. When they reached a two room apartment, his parents approached his aunt. She stood in one corner of the room with folded arms, her face blank and expressionless. As he stood in the doorway, Rupesh heard the adults say something about rent. Frowning, his father waved his son outside. There, he craned his neck to see the birds flying from one palm tree to the next. The familiar sound of quarrelling intruded on his thoughts. Rupesh shivered anxiously and waited.

His father stalked out of the house with a determined look on his hard, sunburned face. He didn't stop to look back at his son. His mother stumbled out and brushed the tears from her eyes, running to catch up to her husband. After a few minutes, she stopped and turned to look at Rupesh one last time. Despite the distance, he could tell that she was crying. She covered her mouth and disappeared behind the trees around the corner. Rupesh froze, his heart pounding as realization swept over his tiny body. He didn't know whether to cry, run after them, or go back to his aunt. He trembled, his vision clouding with tears. A gentle hand touched his shoulder, and he turned to bury his face in his aunt's sari.

Rupesh does not remember much about his life before he came to the Mercy Home. He was six years old when his parents left him with his aunt, and she brought him there that same year. During his first week at the Mercy Home, Rupesh cried and "felt pain deep in his heart". However, as time passed, he began to make friends for the first time. He learned about Jesus Christ and started praying and going to school. Several months later, Rupesh gave his life to the Lord and drank in everything he could about the Word of God. He especially loved the Bible verses about God as his Father and Provider.

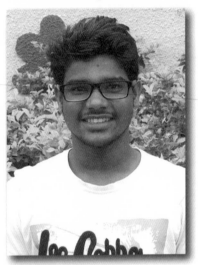

God strengthened Rupesh's new faith by teaching him to pray. When his aunt could not provide clothes for him, he asked God to send him some. Some people from the United States donated clothes to the Mercy Home, and the staff asked the children if anyone needed them. Rupesh raised his hand, and the staff found two outfits that were exactly his size. Rupesh thanked the Lord for providing for his needs. As the time for his 10th grade exams drew closer, Rupesh prayed that God would help him to pass. A passing grade is 35%, and God gave Rupesh an 80%, a score that doubled his request. He didn't have the money for admission into an engineering program, so once again, Rupesh dropped to his knees in prayer. After he had prayed every day for some time, two of the staff members at Mission India's Seminary agreed to sponsor him.

Before he came to the Mercy Home, Rupesh was lonely and illiterate, but now, he is loved and knows the most valuable truth in the world. He dreams of being a mechanical engineer and supporting other children like himself in India. In addition to going to college and serving at the Seminary where he is living, Rupesh teaches math to the 9th-10th graders at the Mercy Home a few times a month. He is praying that God will give him a grateful heart and show him how he can give back to his sponsors and others who have helped him. Although Rupesh does not know where his earthly parents are today, he knows that his heavenly Father will never leave him or forsake him.

Psalm 27:10 - "For my father and my mother have forsaken me, but the Lord will take me up."

Sometimes you may feel like someone has forgotten you. You may wonder if God has forgotten about you or your prayers, but you must remember that He never forgets his children. God did not forget Abraham, Isaac, Jacob, David, or any of the other men of faith. Simeon waited his entire life to see the Messiah, and God kept His promise and allowed Simeon to see and hold the baby Jesus. God listens to your prayers, and though He may not give you the answer that you want, He is taking perfect care of you.

Rupesh teaching and becoming a leader

Good friends in front of the Mercy Home

CHAPTER 5

They Are Weak But He Is Strong

"God uses men who are weak and feeble enough to lean on Him."

— Hudson Taylor, Missionary to China

Gasping for air, Rakesh (pronounced "raw-kesh") placed his hand over his heart and paused on the edge of the gravel road. The cars, motorcycles, and auto rickshaws honked as they crisscrossed the intersection from all directions. Shading his eyes from the bright sun, he spotted his college building about 300 feet away. Sliding into the ditch to avoid a swerving motorcycle, Rakesh began to think about what a miracle it was that he was alive.

Above the noise of the street, Rakesh recalled his neighbor's voice from eighteen years ago: "Your son has a hole in his heart? He will surely die!" His mother had prayed and asked the Hindu gods to heal her baby boy, but they did not answer. In desperation, she had taken her two week old sons to a Christian church service. The pastor had laid his hands on Rakesh's head and called on the name of Jehovah Rapha, the God who heals. One week later, the doctors could not find a single hole in Rakesh's heart! As a result, Rakesh's mother had become a Christian and had raised him to serve the true God. When Rakesh's relatives heard that his mother had converted to Christianity, they told her she was no longer part of their family and could never see them again. The pastor who prayed for Rakesh told his mother that the boys could learn about God and go to school at Mission India's Mercy Home. When she could no longer provide for her boys, she brought them there. Rakesh loved his life at the Mercy Home where he had learned about Jehovah

Rapha, who heals and answers prayer. As he paused to rest against the wall before entering the college, he wondered why he felt so tired and weak.

At three in the afternoon, Rakesh opened the door to his college once again. He had finished his classes for the day and prepared himself for the walk back to the Mercy Home. Computer engineering fascinated him, but he wished that he were stronger. Lifting his eyes towards the blue sky, Rakesh took a deep breath. The coconut palms faded from view as he imagined himself in God's presence. Warmth washed over him as he prayed. "Show me how to live with this pain in my heart. It is small, but every time I walk a few kilometers, I feel tightness in my chest that I don't think should be there. Give me your strength to walk where you want me to go and do what you want me to do. Amen."

Sweating and breathing heavily, Rakesh arrived at the Mercy Home one hour later. He had learned that he had to take slow, measured breaths through his nose to keep himself from fainting. Although he struggled with feeling weak on a daily basis, Rakesh never complained. He loved to play cricket with the other Mercy Home boys and Bible college students, but he knew his limits and rarely ran or over exerted himself. One of the younger boys noticed that Rakesh seemed to be growing weaker and told a staff member about him. As a result, Mission India purchased a bus pass that enabled Rakesh to go to college without placing any extra strain on his body.

The Lord continues to care for his son Rakesh as he is studying for his bachelor's degree in computer engineering. He was baptized in 2012 by his Bible study teacher. As the sun beat down upon his head, Rakesh testified that he had grown to love the Lord Jesus as his personal Father, Provider, and Healer. His favorite Bible verse is Psalm 23:1 because it reminds him that the Lord is his Shepherd and will care for all his physical and spiritual needs. In addition to studying, Rakesh serves on campus in any way he can, often working in the kitchen during conferences. He knows that even though his physical body is weak, the Holy Spirit in him is strong.

> *2 Corinthians 12:9-10 - "And He has said to me, "My grace is sufficient for you, for power is perfected in weakness." Most gladly, therefore, I will rather boast about my weaknesses, so that the power of Christ may dwell in me. Therefore I am well content with weaknesses, with insults, with distresses, with persecutions, with difficulties, for Christ's sake; for when I am weak, then I am strong."*

> *God made each person with different strengths and weaknesses and does not look down on anyone for having a hard time with something. He loves to show his power to help you in your weakness. When you feel like quitting or crying, you can tell Jesus how you feel and ask him to help you to be content during the challenges you face, knowing he is giving you enough grace to get through. God uses these times when you feel weak to teach you that your faith is becoming strong.*

Walking back to the Mercy Home after school

Time for fun - read about Harsh in Chapter 13

CHAPTER 6

You Have The Answer

"Discipline is choosing between what you want now and what you want most."

— *Abraham Lincoln*

Twenty five boys sat on wooden benches at long tables all around him with their heads bent over their books. Surveying the room, Rohit (pronounced "row-heat") counted ten mosquitoes circling above the boy across from him. He began to daydream and recalled his two room house back in Nagpur with its flies and cockroaches. At least the flies and cockroaches didn't bite. As he pictured his mother, his geometry page blurred out of sight and a warm smile lit his face. His mother had left Hinduism to become a Christian after his twin brother was miraculously healed from a heart defect. Rohit's biological father had died two months before they were born, and a few years later, his mother didn't have the money to feed them or pay their school admission fees. Rohit didn't care that they had no furniture and sometimes barely enough rice to eat. All that mattered to him was his mother's presence. Nevertheless, when Rohit and his twin brother Rakesh (pronounced "raw-kesh") were eight years old, she brought them to the Mercy Home and tearfully said goodbye. For the first month that he was there, Rohit cried for his mother every day.

Glancing back down at his geometry book, Rohit thought about how much God had changed him since that first month. Although he had gone to church with his mother as a young child, he did not start to pray by himself until he came to the Mercy Home. Kneeling by his bunk each night, Rohit kept asking God to bring his mother to visit him. God answered his prayers, and his mother visited the twins as frequently as she could. A few years later, she married a man who had also converted to Christianity. Together, they continued to visit the boys.

Closing the textbook, Rohit placed it in his backpack and pulled out his favorite book. Respectfully, Rohit turned the pages of his well-worn Hindi Bible to the book of Matthew, chapter seven. Moving his finger down the page, he read verse seven out loud. "Ask, and it shall be given to you; seek, and you will find. Knock and the door will be opened to you." It was his favorite passage in the Bible. Again and again, he had seen the Lord faithfully keep the promises in this verse. Rohit resolved to do his very best in school and trust God with the results. When the time came to take his nationally ranked tenth grade exams, he prayed this verse again.

Folding his hands, Rohit spoke to his Father. "Jesus, I believe that you hear when I ask and you will answer when I knock. You know how worried I feel about my exams, and how unprepared and incapable I am. Please help me listen to your voice instead of the voice of the enemy who tells me I can't do this. Nothing is too hard for you and you have the answers. In Jesus'  name, Amen." The day that the results were posted, all the students crowded around to see their scores. God had honored his faith and Rohit received the top score in his class!

Now Rohit has new goals and prayers. He is studying at a local community college and working towards his bachelor's degree in business administration. He would like to work for the Indian government as a banker and help other needy children in India. Each morning, he continues to follow Jesus' instructions in Matthew seven and ask God to help him do His will. God really does have the answer for every question!

Matthew 7:7-11 - "Ask, and it will be given to you; seek, and you will find; knock, and it will be opened to you. For everyone who asks receives, and he who seeks finds, and to him who knocks it will be opened. Or what man is there among you who, when his son asks for a loaf, will give him a stone? Or if he asks for a fish, he will not give him a snake, will he? If you then, being evil, know how to give good gifts to your children, how much more will your Father who is in heaven give what is good to those who ask Him!"

You can talk to God every day. The Lord loves to hear everything you have to say. He will never get bored or turn away from you, even after you do something that hurts Him or someone else. God isn't waiting to punish you as soon as you sin. He is the perfect Father, waiting for His children to come and sit on His lap and talk to Him. In Matthew seven, Jesus promises that God the Father gives what is good to those who ask. You can talk to God in prayer as much as you want, and the more you do, you may find that you will trust Him more and worry less.

Mercy Home boys starting a new day

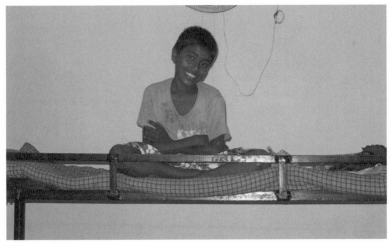

A clean and safe place to sleep

Loving and caring for each other as family members

CHAPTER 7

Unwanted

"Have faith in God. Let God do what He has promised to do. Listen to what He says in His Word and follow it. Even if you can't understand it fully, do it. Believe Him and step out in faith. Faith throws itself onto God and holds Him to His character and His Word. Faith never fails because God never fails."
– K. P. Yohannan, founder of Gospel for Asia

Badal (pronounced "bah-dull") dug his toes into the soft dirt. Wandering around picking up insects and flowers kept him entertained for hours. Spotting a gogel, a red centipede-like insect, he lifted it into the air and stroked its legs. Before his mother died, he used to bring his little creatures home for her inspection. She would admire his discovery, then tickle him and cover his face with kisses. As she was riding her motorcycle home one afternoon, she was hit by a truck and died instantly. The toddler didn't understand why his mother never came home or why his father married Shubam (pronounced "shoe-bomb") shortly thereafter. She hated him without reason and he didn't understand why. Once, when Badal brought her a black cricket, she shrieked and smashed it on the floor. Shubam didn't like little boys who ran around and talked to her all day long. How he ached for his own dear mother with her loving smiles and warm embrace! Gently, Badal placed the gogel on a twig.

Rising from his seat on the large bitter gourd leaves, Badal attempted to brush the dirt off of his feet. Shubam would be angry with him if he tracked mud into their three room house. Sliding down the slope, Badal's bare feet smacked onto the paved road. He skirted the ditch as he skipped back home, wondering if his father was driving any of the government cars that sped past him. When Badal entered his house, his half-brother Viraj (pronounced "vee-rawj") was dangling his foot over the side of the metal bed frame as he worked on his homework. Since Badal was only three, he slept on the floor, but he didn't mind. After all, almost everyone ate on the floor and families often slept there too. Steam wafted through the room as Shubam removed the lid from the rice. Viraj and Badal ran into the kitchen. Shubam shooed Badal away, insisting dinner wasn't ready and he was dirty. Shyly, Badal went outside and spent the next half hour turning over stones and searching for gogels.

When he came back inside, Shubam was washing the rice and curry off their dinner plates and talking with his father Raju (pronounced "raw-joo"). She did not care that she had kept Badal from eating. He could hear Shubam pressuring his father, but Raju seemed undecided about something. They had heard about Mission India's Mercy Home, and Shubam wouldn't stop pushing until Raju agreed to take his son there. Now looking from his father to his stepmother, Badal realized they were talking about sending him away. Surely his father loved him and had ample means to take care of him; would his father convince her to keep him? Weakly, Raju reasoned with Shubam, but several minutes later, he caved in and agreed to take Badal to the Mercy Home. A few days later, Shubam folded Badal's two outfits and secured them in a small knapsack on his back. He wore his only pair of sandals. Raju brought Badal to the Mercy Home and left without a word.

Badal felt unwanted and unloved. He had been betrayed by his own father. Tears coursed down his cheeks day after day as he watched the other children play in front of the Mercy Home. Each time Molly Auntie found Badal crying, she picked him up and held him close. Her tender love, combined with the consistent meals he received, opened his heart again. Soon, Badal was catching gogels for Molly Auntie and running around with the other boys. As the years passed, Badal completed his high school requirements and grew in his knowledge of God. After his baptism in 2015, Badal became a leader at the Mercy Home. He led evening devotions, ran errands for the staff, and oversaw the younger boys in his room.

"What happened?" Badal questioned gently, looking down at a little boy who had folded himself into a little heap on the sidewalk. Crouching down on the cement, Badal tenderly stroked his back and motioned for the offender. Sheepishly, Ashish (pronounced "uh-sheesh") related that the younger boy had refused to give him some

sticks, and then admitted that he had angrily crushed the child's sand creation. A few boys stood in a semi-circle and waited to hear Badal's response. Calmly, Badal asked Ashish how he would feel if someone crushed his sand hut, and what Jesus would want him to do next. Ashish apologized, the little boy forgave him, and Badal rose to his feet.

"Come play cricket with us, Badal!" someone shouted. "You have to practice if you want to become a professional cricketer..." he grinned persuasively.

"Badal, I want you to be on my team!" Ashish called, leaving his sand hut and seizing Badal's hand.

"No, Badal is on my team!" another boy hollered, swinging a wicket above his head. Laughing, Badal ran to join the boys who were gathering in the middle of the field. Badal loved competition, and he was a respected teammate and leader.

The boy who was rejected as a toddler is now surrounded by

people who love him. Although Badal is only sixteen years old, he is already taking college classes in the nearby city and working at the Mercy Home. When he is not busy, the younger children love to spend time sitting, eating, and playing with him. Badal remembers the time when he was a lonely child and how God saved him and taught him about unconditional love. The Lord provided for Badal when he was unwanted and changed his tears into laughter.

Psalm 30:11 "You have turned for me my mourning into dancing; You have loosed my sackcloth and girded me with gladness."

God can take anyone's sadness and turn it into joy. God cares about you even when you may feel like no one else does. Never forget that no matter how bad your situation is or how helpless you feel, God cares about you. He will give you something good even from the bad things in your life.

Cricket with friends

CHAPTER 8
Worth Saving

"I have but one candle of life to burn, and I would rather burn it in a land filled with darkness than in a land flooded with lights."

— Ion Keith-Falconer,
Missionary to the Arabian Peninsula

Smoke enveloped the hut. As the tin roof started to melt, the toxic fumes sucked the remaining oxygen from the room. The walls, consisting of dried mud piles, bundles of sticks, and a few cloth sheets, were rapidly disappearing. In a few minutes, the hut would collapse inwards, swallowed by the flames.

"Over here...hurry!" a young boy gasped for air as he directed the policeman to the burning hut.

"Is anyone inside? Who lives here?" called the village policeman.

"Just a young widow and her three small girls. They're worthless members of a lower caste. Their death means nothing to us." An elderly man scowled, spitting on the ground as if it was disgusting to talk about them.

Ignoring the villager's cruel remark, the policeman pushed past the growing crowd and leapt inside the burning hut. He recognized the smell of gas and realized that someone had purposefully set it on fire. Crawling around on his hands and knees, he searched for the widow and her three girls. As he started to cough and choke on the fumes, he bumped into a crib. Baby Nikita (pronounced "nick-ee-tah") was sleeping in the crib. Grabbing the child, the brave officer dragged her out of the hut. As he lay on the ground catching his breath with the infant beside him, the hut collapsed. The hair on the six-month-old's head and arms had been burned, but she was safe.

"Taking your new job seriously, are you?" the elderly man scoffed, when he saw the young policeman bending over the child. "It's a girl? Next time you risk your life, risk it for someone who is worth saving. Look at that dirty beggar; she won't live for a month! You'd be a fool to keep her." He shuffled away, shaking his head in disbelief.

Undaunted, the policeman squared his shoulders and returned to the police station with the baby girl cradled in his arms. The tiny station was about the size of a two-car garage. It had three tiny jail cells, a room with a cot, and a small bathroom locked behind an iron gate. The policeman unlocked the gate and put Nikita to sleep on the cot. Locking the gate behind him, he sat down at his desk. Posters papered the walls and several plastic chairs completed his office. He knew that Nikita's mother had died in the fire, but he wondered what happened to her unfortunate sisters.

Several hours later, two frightened young girls came into the police station. While the two girls fidgeted nervously, the compassionate policeman got out his notebook and asked them to tell their story. Six-year-old Sonu (pronounced "so-new") claimed that their father had left them before Nikita was born. Their mother had begun to cook and wash for neighbors, but because she was born into a lower caste, no one would pay her enough money to buy food. Sonu and four-year-old Kalpana (pronounced "call-pun-nuh") had become tired of staying in their hut with empty stomachs and nothing to do. While their mother worked, they ran around the village from morning until evening. That particular evening, the sisters had returned home only to find that their hut had been burned. A sympathetic neighbor boy had heard them crying and brought them to the police station.

After Sonu finished telling her story, the officer told the sisters to wait while he got something from the back of the station. Kalpana started to cry and Sonu lifted her onto her lap and rocked her back and forth. They didn't know what would happen to them next. The policeman returned carrying baby Nikita. He told the girls about the fire, their mother's death, and how he was able to save Nikita just in time. Kalpana jumped out of Sonu's arms and pulled the man's arm down so she could see her baby sister. Sonu swallowed her tears and asked if she could hold Nikita. Tenderly, the man handled the bundle to Sonu and watched the sisters. Bravely, Sonu assured her sisters that they would be fine; somehow she would find a place for them to sleep together and look for food in the morning.

Moved with pity, the policeman invited the girls to live at the police station. He promised take care of them as long as they would listen and stay in the safety of the station until he found someone to adopt them. With tears streaming down her cheeks, Sonu gratefully accepted his generous offer. Kalpana walked over to the officer and wrapped her tiny arms around his leg. They did not know that God was intervening in their lives.

Several months later, baby Nikita and her sisters were adopted by a kind Hindu family. The family paid for the sisters to live at a small hostel for girls where they could get an education. Nikita and her sisters lived on the main floor of the hostel with about twenty other girls. Upstairs, the warden and his family furnished classrooms where several teachers could come each day to tutor the girls. The food was watery and the girls had to sleep on the floor, but they were grateful to be at the hostel. When Nikita was in fourth grade, her adopted father left the family, and her adopted mother could not afford to keep the girls at the hostel. In the midst of the upheaval, Nikita's adopted grandfather became a Christian. He met a pastor who told him about the Mercy Home and then decided to send the girls to live there.

Nikita and her sisters moved to the Mercy Home when she was ten years old. There, they all heard the gospel for the first time. Nikita recounted how Joseph, the Mercy Home warden at the time, had cared for her like she was his own daughter. She remembers how he used to play jump rope and other games with the children during their free time. Although she had received daily Christian teaching at the Mercy Home, Nikita did not commit her life to Christ until she was fifteen years old. While she was praying one evening, God touched her heart and told her how much He loved her. After that, Nikita talked to God about all her problems and her joys. She told Jesus about the things that made her laugh and the things that confused her at school. When she needed new clothes, she prayed and waited for God to send them to her. Sonu, who had left the Mercy Home and married a Hindu man, sent Nikita some clothes. The Lord was with Nikita, providing for her and leading her.

Nikita now enjoys spending time with children and believes that God is leading her to become a teacher. In June 2016, Nikita moved from the Mercy Home to the girls' dormitory with other Bible college students. Currently, she is taking courses for her

teacher's certificate at a secular college as well as Bible classes at Mission India Theological Seminary. Her sister Kalpana is also living in the girls' dormitory and taking Bible classes at the seminary. The Hindu family that adopted Nikita and her sisters when they were younger stopped supporting them financially and has not communicated with them in several years. It is common for a family to stop supporting children after one of the siblings gets married. The eldest is responsible to care for his parents and younger siblings. Nikita and Kalpana are trusting God to give them everything they need for their studies and living expenses.

Nikita is precious in God's sight. Contrary to what the villager said when Nikita's hut was burned, she is not a worthless beggar; she is loved by her Creator. Her favorite Scripture passage is Jeremiah

33:2-3: *"Thus says the Lord who made the earth, the Lord who formed it to establish it, the Lord is His name, 'Call to Me and I will answer you, and I will tell you great and mighty things, which you do not know.'"* She says, "It reminds me that in all difficult situations, when I pray and ask for help, Jesus answers." The King of heaven rescued her out of the fire of hell in order to show His power in her life.

Psalm 72:12-14 - "For he will deliver the needy when he cries for help, the afflicted also, and him who has no helper. He will have compassion on the poor and needy, and the lives of the needy he will save. He will rescue their life from oppression and violence, and their blood will be precious in his sight."

God made all the people in this world and they are all valuable to Him. When you believe what God says in the Bible about the value of people, God gives you the strength to choose to treat everyone as valuable and priceless.

Three happy little ladies

Nutrition is one of the keys to health and education

Girls walking to school. Over 18% of females are married by the age of 15 and 47% are married by the age of 18 in India.

CHAPTER 9

From Confusion To Comfort

"The real calling is not to a certain place or career, but to everyday obedience. That call is extended to every Christian, not just a selected few."
— *Brother Andrew, Bible Smuggler and Founder of Open Doors USA*

Seven year old Sonali (pronounced "so-nah-lee") loved helping her mother. Together, they washed their clay pots, scrubbed their clothes on a large rock, and drew water from the village well. Her brother and sister preferred to play in the village, but she was content to be with her mother. The families in Sonali's village had to travel 6 kilometers (or 3.72 miles) to the city to buy vegetables and rice. Sonali especially loved walking to the city with her mother, but they were unaware that someone was watching them.

While they were making curry one day, Sonali and her mother were startled to see a stranger come into their house. Immediately, Sonali sensed that he was dangerous and ran to her mother to protect her. The evil man grabbed a hard table fan and beat Sonali over the head with it until she fell unconscious on the floor. About an hour later, Sonali woke up and looked around her two-room home. Her pounding headache reminded her of what happened. Her mother was gone! She had been kidnapped, and although her father had searched for his wife, she had completely vanished.

Since her mother was gone, her father quickly arranged another marriage. He needed someone to care for his children, but he soon discovered that his new wife had a mental problem that left her unable to complete basic tasks. He contracted tuberculosis, but did not have the money to buy the medicine he needed. Sadly, when Sonali was only eight years old, her father died and his new wife went back to her family. Sonali had no idea how to take care of her siblings all by herself. Despondently, Sonali's brother and sister wandered around the village begging for food. Since she didn't like to ask other people for things, Sonali usually went hungry. Their situation became more and more desperate.

Curling up in the corner of their mud house, Sonali hugged her knees to her chest. A cool wind was blowing through the trees, and the last rays of sunlight were sinking into the horizon. If she couldn't eat anything, at least she could stay warm in this position. A shadow fell across the threshold and someone entered the house. She glanced up and cried out in surprise. Her mother had miraculously returned! Apparently, the kidnapper was a witch doctor who had used black magic to cast a spell that had temporarily confused her mother's

mind and blocked all memories of her family. Sonali was thrilled to be with her mother again. They wondered how the spell had worn off and how she had escaped and found her way back to her children. However, no matter how hard they worked, the little family barely had enough food to keep from starving. One month after Sonali's mother returned, her uncle heard about their situation. He could see no other solution, and brought nine-year-old Sonali and her sister to live at the Mercy Home.

For the first time, Sonali could relax and did not worry about what she would eat the next day. She grew stronger from the regular diet and gradually became able to play with the other girls. Molly Auntie, the Mercy Home warden, spent time cooking and talking with Sonali. The more she learned about Christ, the more she felt at peace.

Sonali no longer feels worried about where her next meal will come from because she has found that Jesus provides for her. She says, "Here, I learned that Jesus is my Shepherd; He is very careful to care for me and look out for me." After completing her two year science diploma, she is pursuing her bachelor's degree in theology at Mission India Theological Seminary. God is teaching her how to love others as Christ loved us, and consider them before herself. Her goal is to become a nurse and help people like her father. Sonali looks forward to the future because she knows that her Shepherd will lead and provide for her.

Psalm 23:1-4 - "The Lord is my shepherd, I shall not want. He makes me lie down in green pastures; He leads me beside quiet waters. He restores my soul; He guides me in the paths of righteousness for His name's sake. Even though I walk through the valley of the shadow of death, I fear no evil, for you are with me; Your rod and your staff, they comfort me."

If you are a child of God, Jesus is your Shepherd. You may worry that you will not have enough of what you need, but somehow, the Lord will provide for you. No evil can touch you without God's permission. Because of what Jesus did on the cross, there is a shield around every one of His children that all of hell cannot break. God has given you the instructions you need to make wise choices in His word the Bible. The Holy Spirit will remind you to make right choices that honor God and put others before yourself. He will lead you and care for you as you follow Christ.

Mercy Home girls preparing food for the next meal

*Time for children
to be children*

CHAPTER 10

Respect And Responsibility

"I am created to magnify the glory of God. Not the way that a microscope magnifies (making small things look bigger than they are), but the way a telescope magnifies (making things that appear small to the world look as gigantic as they really are)."

— John Piper, Founder and
Teacher of Desiring God

Stopping to catch his breath, Rohit (pronounced "row-heat") gripped his side. He was tired from playing tag with the village boys. A low growl reminded Rohit that he hadn't eaten since dawn. The sun shot pink, orange, and purple rays through the trees and the parrots flying overhead seemed to call him home. Calling over his shoulder to tell his playmates he was leaving, Rohit turned his footsteps home. When he passed his father's shop, he paused and craned his neck to see if his father was in the back. The store was empty. With a heavy sigh, the nine year old boy continued on his way. As he passed the liquor store, Rohit thought he heard his father's deep voice. Sure enough, his father was reclining on a wooden stool surrounded by several other men. Lowering his head, Rohit stared at the ground and quickened his pace along the muddy streets of Nagpur.

When he reached his grandparents' home, Rohit heard a strange voice inside the cement room. Ducking inside, he sat down near the wall and listened. His grandmother was talking to a woman who lived down the street. Not wishing to interrupt his elders, Rohit crawled over to the pot of rice and scooped a large handful onto a banana leaf plate. As he blew on the rice to cool it off, his stomach growled loudly. The ladies turned around and saw him.

"See, what did I tell you? The boy is starved for a good life. I know you are giving him everything you can, but I found a better place for him." The visitor nodded compassionately in Rohit's direction.

"You're right; Rohit spends all day roaming the streets with the village boys. I am concerned for his safety; I don't want those boys to lead him into trouble." His grandmother looked anxiously at her young grandson and lowered her voice before continuing. "My son argued with Rohit's mother constantly. She didn't like his drinking habits. One day after my son left the house in a rage, my husband decided to end the disrespectful behavior in his family. He burned Rohit's mother while the boy was out with his friends. I felt sorry for the child and brought him to live with us. I know that Rohit is deathly afraid of his grandfather and leaves the house to avoid him."

The elder woman hung her head and covered her mouth with her hand. Rohit guessed that she was talking about him and inched closer so he could hear the conversation. To his surprise, the younger woman gave his grandmother a quick hug.

"Trust me," she assured the elder lady, "Rohit will be safe at the Mercy Home. The Christians there will give him everything he needs and he can go to school. I will take him there if you and your husband will give me permission."

Rohit arrived at the Mercy Home two weeks later. At first, he wasn't sure he liked the schedule, but in a few weeks, he began to look forward to school, study, and play time. He quickly made friends with the other boys and became one of their best cricket players. Since his family followed the Jain religion, Rohit had never heard the gospel before. During chapel and Sunday school, he drank in the stories about Jesus' miracles and love for His children. He received a Bible and started to read it for himself. Jesus Christ showed him that He was the one who had protected him from evil and chosen him to be His child. Rohit came to understand that Jesus paid the debt for everything that he thought, said and did. Even though his earthly father was not responsible for him, Rohit learned that Jesus is always faithful.

Rohit sees that Jesus has given him a much better life than he ever imagined. Although he is only sixteen, he is respected by the younger Mercy Home boys as a firm and gentle leader. He loves to play cricket and wonders if he could be a professional cricket player. He said, "Even though I ran around with the village boys, I used to be so lonely. I had no brothers and sisters and my father ignored me. Then I came to the Mercy Home where I was surrounded by children. I am so thankful that God brought me here. Jesus changed my life." His responsibility and obedience is a result of God's work in his life.

Colossians 3:23-24 - "Whatever you do, do your work heartily, as for the Lord rather than for men, knowing that from the Lord you will receive the reward of the inheritance. It is the Lord Christ whom you serve."

We can be glad to complete the tasks that God has given us to do. When you have any kind of job to do, whether large or small, do your best. Smile and work quickly and thoroughly. Remember that Jesus is helping you and watching over you. God loves to see your cheerful attitude, and you can show your love for Jesus by the way you care about the little jobs He gives you to do.

Mercy Home's dormitory style bedrooms

Ready for daily chapel at the Mercy Home

CHAPTER 11
He Will Carry Me

"Prayer; secret, fervent, believing prayer, lies at the root of all personal godliness."
— William Carey, Missionary to India

Paralyzed with shock, she stared at the scene before her. She tried to scream, but her mouth was completely dry. Her throat became so swollen that she could barely feel the air fill her lungs when she breathed in. The horrific image was imprinted on her mind forever. Staggering backwards, she nearly lost her balance. A wave of nausea surged through her thin body. Three miles lay between her and the place where her mother was working; a long distance for a five year old to travel. Although it was not yet six o'clock in the morning, men were outside herding animals, smoking, or preparing their shop stalls. Women were cooking rice over a small fire pit or packing things to sell in the market or take to work. It would be dangerous for her to go alone, but she had to take the risk and hope she wouldn't be abducted. Swallowing the lump that threatened to suffocate her, Akanksha (pronounced "ah-conk-shah") clenched her skirt in both fists and ran.

Across the garbage piles, over the cement, through the muddy alleys, along the barbed wire fence, on the rocky path she flew. As the jagged stones cut her feet, she realized she wasn't wearing her sandals. That didn't matter now. She had to reach her mother as quickly as possible. The rows of tin shacks and straw huts grew thin as she crossed the stream into the field. The tall grass whipped her legs and arms as she shoved them out of her way. As the sun climbed above the trees, Akanksha remembered her younger sister and trembled violently. If Sanskruti (pronounced "sawn-screw-tea") or Aryan (pronounced "are-ee-on") woke up and went outside, there was no telling what the toddlers would do or where they might go in their panic. The memory of her younger siblings' faces brought tears to her eyes. She almost paused to cry, but adrenaline propelled her forward. Her legs felt like jelly, but she continued to run, half shuffling, through the field. It took every ounce of strength in her body to take another step, but terror urged her on.

Reaching the edge of the field, Akanksha saw the row of tin houses and smoke rising from the place where her mother worked. Akanksha's mother made incense sticks that Hindu worshippers use during sacrifices and prayer time. The aroma of incense and essential oils overwhelmed her as she crumpled into a heap on the doorstep. Akanksha stirred as her mother touched her bleeding feet. Her entire body felt numb and her head spun with agony.

"Mother," she choked, "father finally did it…" the words died on her lips.

The color drained from her mother's face as she realized what Akanksha was saying.

"All I wanted was to be the first one to ride the swing he promised us, but this morning…" Akanksha sobbed uncontrollably. Tenderly, her mother pulled Akanksha into her arms and stroked her heaving back.

When she could breathe again, the little girl finished. "There's no swing, just father hanging from the rope."

A year later, Akanksha's mother heard about the Mercy Home, and sent Akanksha and her sister to live there. After her mother's death, Akanksha's aunt agreed to support them. However, her aunt was Hindu, and threatened that if the girls ever became Christians, she would cut off all communication with them. In Indian culture, children must ask their parents or relatives before making a major decision. Akanksha longed to be baptized, but felt she must ask her aunt's permission first.

Fifteen year old Akanksha eagerly focused on her Sunday school teacher. It was here in this room where Akanksha had heard the gospel for the first time. Grinning, she breathed a silent prayer of thanks to the Lord. Glancing behind her, she caught Sanskruti whispering to her friend. Another orphan, Payal (pronounced "pile"), sat in front of her. Akanksha suppressed the giggle that rose in her throat when she thought about Payal. She remembered how they used to argue several years ago, but now they had both accepted Christ and had become inseparable prayer partners. Pulling her scarf over her head again in reverence for God, Akanksha bowed her head and folded her hands. The teacher started the lesson with a prayer and then instructed the children to pray for someone they knew who did not know Christ. Instantly, Akanksha thought about her aunt.

"Lord," she prayed, "open her heart to see you. Show her that you are the only true God, and that you will carry her just as you have carried me. Give me the wisdom to know how to respond to her

and the patience to wait for baptism until you show me it's the right time. I will have my tenth standard exams this year and I want to pass for your glory. You know I want to be a doctor and I will need to take further studies. Please provide for me either through my aunt or a sponsor so I can continue to serve you. You are my shelter and my fortress, my God in whom I trust. Amen."

Although Akanksha was an orphan from the world's perspective, she had found more family members than she could count in the body of Christ. As Akanksha lifted her head from prayer, she smiled and looked at all the children around her who were praying for their family members, adopted parents, teachers, and friends. She thanked the Lord for carrying her safely to the Mercy Home and answering her prayers.

Psalm 28:7-9 - "The Lord is my strength and my shield; my heart trusts in Him, and I am helped; therefore my heart exults, and with my song I shall thank Him. The Lord is their strength, and He is a saving defense to His anointed. Save your people and bless your inheritance; be their shepherd also, and carry them forever."

Do you trust in the Lord to carry you through the problems in your life? Do you thank the Lord for everything that he has given you and pray for those who do not know Jesus? You can start today. Pray that God will give you a caring heart for the people around you and pray for the Christians in India.

CHAPTER 12
A Plate Of Food

The Bible is full of ordinary people who went to impossible places and did wondrous things simply because they decided to obey God."
— Brother Andrew, Bible Smuggler and Founder of Open Doors USA

"Don't ask me again, I told you, I'm not hungry." Sanskruti (pronounced "sawn-screw-tea") folded her arms deliberately across her chest. Undeterred, Eshwari (pronounced "eesh-wah-ree"), one of the older girls living at the Mercy Home, calmly served Sanskruti a large pile of rice, dahl (a type of lentil stew; pronounced "doll"), and curry. Stubbornly, Sanskruti pushed the plate away and laid her head on the table. The horrible scene broke into her thoughts again. She saw her father hanging from the tree in her front yard, her mother and older sister Akanksha (pronounced "ah-conk-shah") wailing, and her little brother clinging to her skirt in bewilderment. She let out a quiet cry and quickly covered her face with her hands. Although she desperately wanted to forget it, the nightmare of her father's suicide haunted her at least twice a day. She had grown to expect it, but that didn't lessen the pain she felt with each recurring memory. Bitterly, Sanskruti thought that she did not have a single friend who understood her pain. Gently, Eshwari placed a hand on her shoulder. Sanskruti ignored her. She did not believe that anyone could care about her.

Uncle Joseph, the Mercy Home warden at the time, summoned Sanskruti and her sister. "Akanksha, Sanskruti, come. Your cousin is here to take you home."

When she looked into her cousin's cold, stern eyes, Sanskruti's little heart shrank back. She took Akanksha's hand and followed her older relative timidly. As the three crossed the threshold, Sanskruti turned to see Eshwari smile sympathetically and blow her a kiss.

When they arrived at Sanskruti's house, she deliberately closed her eyes so she would not see the tree where her father committed suicide. Inside, the girls were surprised to see many adults huddled around a bed in the corner of the room, speaking in hushed tones. Grimly, her cousin escorted the sisters to the bedside and motioned for the others to move aside. He hadn't said a word to the girls about why they were coming home. They were completely unprepared for the sight that met their eyes. A woman lay motionless on the bed, her scar-covered body bearing witness to her brutal death. Squinting to adjust her eyes to the darkness of the room, Sanskruti cautiously peered at the woman's face. It was her mother. Screaming at the top of her lungs, Sanskruti fled from the house, and out onto the road. She didn't care what happened to her; she just wanted to escape from the new nightmare. One of her aunts caught up with her and pulled the sobbing child back into the house. Akanksha had passed out on the dirt floor. Having informed the girls, the adults then debated what to do with them next.

As the wooden cart rattled up the driveway three days later, Sanskruti stared blankly at the Mercy Home building. Now she was an orphan. Vaguely, Sanskruti remembered Joseph speaking with the driver, then hugging her and Akanksha and leading them to their room. Throwing herself down on her bunk bed, Sanskruti wrapped herself into a ball and wept.

As the days passed, she continued to refuse food. She stayed in her room or huddled in corners while the other children played. Eshwari soon learned the tragic news of how Sanskruti's mother was burnt to death by a man she had trusted and called brother after her husband's death. She sympathized with Sanskruti and longed to help her find peace and healing from the Lord. At every meal, she brought food to Sanskruti in her room. They would sit together in complete silence, while Eshwari waited patiently with a compassionate expression on her face. Sanskruti couldn't express the grief and numbness she felt. Her nightmares and apathy had doubled, yet Eshwari continued to reach out to her. The younger girl couldn't understand why Eshwari loved her, because all she did was refuse her kind gestures.

Just then, the dinner bell clanged, interrupting Sanskruti's musings. Eshwari came in bearing a steaming plate of rice and curry and plopped down on Sanskruti's bed. Tenderly, she put her arm around the younger girl's thin shoulders and tucked her hair behind her ears. Sanskruti burst into tears. As she comforted her friend, Eshwari told Sanskruti how Jesus is more than a father and mother and He can never die. He conquered death when He rose from the dead and He is preparing a place for all His adopted children in heaven where tears and pain can never enter. Eshwari's faithfulness and patience in sharing God's love had finally melted the bars of depression and unlocked the door to Sanskruti's heart.

A few months later, Sanskruti leaned forward to hear Nikita (pronounced "Nick-ee-tah"), speak. Nikita was one of the students at Mission India Theological Seminary, and she taught Sanskruti's Sunday school class.

"You are the children; you have the energy and time to enjoy life. The adults around you have so much to worry about and take care of. When they look at your face, they want to see your bright joyful smile."

The students giggled and eyed each other shyly while their teacher continued.

"You are like a flower growing by the side of the road. The flower is bright and beautiful, and people expect it to share its sweet fragrance. If you are not happy, you are like a flower that refuses to show its face or share its sweetness with anyone."

Sanskruti grinned as she pictured herself growing in a ditch as a purple flower.

"Even if you do not feel happy, when you smile, your attitude will change and others will be attracted to your light. It is our duty as children and young people to smile at others. With your smile and love, others will come to know Jesus and the peace he gives his children. Do you understand?"

The students assented, and Nikita closed the Sunday school lesson in prayer. As Sanskruti bowed her head, she resolved to be cheerful, no matter how she felt. She believed God would give her joy, just as he had healed her from the pain of losing her parents.

Sanskruti is in ninth grade now and dreams of serving people as a doctor. Nikita's words have made a lasting impact on Sanskruti and her sister Akanksha. Both girls beam radiantly whenever they greet someone, and the teenagers are reaching out to the younger girls at the Mercy Home. Sanskruti is learning how to lead by example. She says, "I didn't feel God loving me on my own. I didn't feel it when I read my Bible or heard the gospel at church. The first time I felt God's love was when the Christians at the Mercy Home loved me. Because of them, I wanted to know Jesus."

Matthew 10:42 – "And whoever in the name of a disciple gives to one of these little ones even a cup of cold water to drink, truly I say to you, he shall not lose his reward."

Jesus said that whatever you do for another person, you have done for Him. You might think that your job is very small, or that you're too young to help God, but even your smile can make a difference in someone's life. Choose to be kind to others whenever you can.

CHAPTER 13
I Want To Go Home

"Once you become aware that the main business that you are here for is to know God, most of life's problems fall into place of their own accord."

– J. I. Packer

Harsh stirred the coals under the iron pot. The fragrant steam wafted through the air as the tea continued to boil. An elderly woman sat beside him with a small pitcher of fresh milk. She had cared for him since his infancy. Peering into the pot, Harsh thought about his mother and sighed. His grandmother poured the milk into the tea and squeezed his hand.

"Your mother was a beautiful, strong, woman. You look just like her, my son."

Harsh couldn't help but wonder why his parents had died. His mother passed away barely one hour after his birth. His father, overwhelmed with grief at his wife's death, threw himself to alcohol to escape his pain. His father became a hopeless addict, often wandering to his sister's home and beating her at all hours of the day and night. His aunt had enrolled Harsh in a Christian hostel and school when he was in first grade. She found comfort knowing that Harsh was safe at the hostel. Then, Harsh's father contracted jaundice, a disease that causes liver failure. The last image Harsh had of his father was of his father's ashen face before it was covered with dirt at his burial.

He was interrupted from his memories by the gentle touch of his grandmother's hand on his shoulder. Without a word, she handed him a small glass of tea and stroked his back knowingly. Harsh's sharp ears detected footsteps approaching and turned towards the sound. His grandmother was starting to lose her hearing, but with Harsh beside her, she felt secure.

Durga, a tall, slender girl of fifteen, joined her cousin and grandmother on the straw mat.

"School was exhausting. I'm trying to understand the grammar, but it's so difficult!" The girl's voice hinted at her frustration. Grandmother rose to get another cup, and Harsh stared at the floor. Durga's quick eyes noticed her cousin's change of attitude at the mention of school.

She smirked saucily and added, "Harsh will be going back to school in just a few days. Then he can try his hand at grammar and see if he wants to complain, too." Durga sipped her tea and studied Harsh's face. His crestfallen posture and expression pained the elder woman's heart. She couldn't bear to part with him; he was husband, son, and grandson to her. Just then, Harsh's aunt entered the room.

"Mother, don't you think it will be good for Harsh to go back to the hostel and continue his studies?" Durga questioned innocently. Harsh hugged his knees to his chest and held his breath. His aunt cleared her throat before accepting her cup of tea and joining the family on the mat.

"Actually, I have been thinking about that hostel. I do not think it is very safe. Monsoon has been particularly severe this year, and the lake outside the hostel is higher than ever. I am concerned that Harsh may be carried away in the current while he is playing."

"Mother, we cannot live forever off of the small sum you are making cleaning other homes. Soon we will have to sell our bed, and it's the only piece of furniture we have. I don't know how we are able to pay school fees as it is. Maybe if Harsh doesn't want to study, he can find a job and start to work." Durga didn't intend to sound unkind, but Harsh became increasingly fearful and apprehensive.

"I don't want to study. I don't want to go back to that place. I don't want to leave grandmother, either," the twelve year old murmured.

"You have to study if you don't want to become like your father. He was just a rickshaw driver. But go ahead, suit yourself. Just don't drink and ruin your life. We all need you to provide for us." Durga finished and watched her cousin. Eyebrows twitching, chest heaving to steady his breath, hands trembling, Harsh rose to his feet and headed for the stairs.

The roof was Harsh's favorite part of the cement house. Scrambling to the top and swallowing the lump that repeatedly rose in his throat, the boy swung his legs over the edge and tried to focus on the glowing horizon. It was hard to keep his balance when his whole body was shaking with emotion. As the hot tears trickled down his face, he saw his grandmother out of the corner of his eye. The dear lady had braved the difficult climb up to the roof to comfort him. The shadows lengthened as the pair gazed at the city below them. Her left arm wrapped around his shoulder while his hands clutched her right hand. If only that moment could last forever.

The sun rose the following morning and climbed higher in the sky, threatening to scorch the child who dared to sweep under its rays. Beads of sweat ran down Harsh's back as he pushed the broom made of coconut fronds around in front of his house.

His Aunt Lakshmi's voice wafted through the stuffy air. "Harsh! Mother! Come!"

Her excitement made Harsh's heart stand still for a few seconds. He dropped the broom and joined his grandmother and aunt in the dim house. Lakshmi described how she had met a man named Vikas (pronounced "why-cause") while she was purchasing more cleaning supplies in the market. Vikas was a Christian who worked at Mission India. After hearing of their situation, he asked her to consider sending Harsh to Mission India's Mercy Home. There, he had assured her, Harsh would receive high quality care and education. As she spoke, Harsh glanced up at his grandmother for support.

Lakshmi concluded, "We are Hindu, but Christian education lays an excellent foundation in moral training and will help Harsh live a better life after his reincarnation. I am going to visit the Mercy Home, but I have already decided that we should send him there for the school year."

Two days later, Harsh clung to his grandmother as they approached the Mercy Home. He liked the grounds, and the boys seemed kind. He brightened when he saw one of the boys motion for him to join the cricket game. The next few hours felt like a blur. Grandmother spoke with Molly Auntie while one of the older boys gave Harsh a tour and introduced him to his room leader. After dinner, the children gathered in the main room for a special program from the Bible college students. The students performed a skit based off of a Bible story, and their antics caused Harsh to laugh like he hadn't laughed in years. The action songs were his favorite, and by a few weeks later, Harsh had memorized all the hand motions in Sunday school.

Although Harsh enjoyed his new life at the Mercy Home, he ached for his grandmother. He had heard about Jesus at the other Christian hostel, but there were so many children there that the staff did not have time to talk to all of them. Harsh had done as he pleased at the first hostel with little supervision. While the people at the Mercy Home were very kind to him and the schedule allowed him to work, play, and study, something was missing. The now thirteen year old boy wondered if the Christian God was real. It felt like He was far away.

Vaibhav (pronounced "way-bo") tapped Harsh's shoulder. "Trouble studying again?" the older boy asked playfully. Harsh blushed and shook his head in agreement.

"Tell me what's wrong, Harsh." His genuine concern brought tears to Harsh's eyes. Deliberately, he squared his shoulders and clenched his teeth to prevent them from chattering.

"No interest. I do not care about my studies right now." He shuffled his feet under the wooden bench. The other boys glanced up from their books to look at Harsh, and then dutifully returned to their work. Harsh felt bad, but he wanted to be honest.

Vaibhav touched his hand. "I thought you wanted to become a teacher for small children, Harsh. You would be a wonderful teacher." Harsh couldn't control himself any longer.

"I miss my grandmother!" he declared, and hastily gathering his books, he headed to his bedroom.

"Grace Didi, Harsh does not want to stay at the Mercy Home." One of the girls tugged on Grace's sleeve. "Please talk to him; he likes to be with you; so maybe you can make him understand."

Concerned, Grace wondered how she could help. This dear boy seemed joyful, but distant. Something was weighing on his heart in the back of his mind even while he was playing. When free time finished and all the students sat down at their assigned benches for study hour, Grace approached Harsh's table.

Harsh's face lit up when he saw her. "Didi, please sit with me."

He nudged the boy beside him, and they made space for her to sit down. Grace treasured the title "Didi" because it means "older sister" in Hindi. Harsh casually turned the pages of his English vocabulary notebook. His neat handwriting caught Grace's attention, and she praised him for his orderliness. Beaming, the boy showed her several pages where he had carefully measured columns of words that he needed to study. Intuitively, she asked him to describe what the words meant in English. Some of the words he knew right away, but others he hesitated to define, then tried to dismiss her by saying that he only knew a little bit of English. Laughing, she urged him to keep trying. Together, they spent the entire hour explaining various words to each other in a mixture of English and Hindi.

Harsh begged Grace to come back the following evening to study with him again. She rearranged her schedule and returned the next evening to look at his vocabulary book. Pointing to the word "study," Grace waited for Harsh to explain it in Hindi. Harsh searched for words, then grinned and waved his arms to communicate that the two of them were actively demonstrating the word. When Grace asked him if he wanted to study, Harsh's face fell. Shifting his weight and surveying the room, Harsh attempted to hide the tears that clouded his vision.

Turning to Grace, he said, "Didi, remember how you told me that I remind you of your brother David? You miss David, yes? I have no father or mother, only grandmother." Harsh gulped and gripped Grace's arm for support. "My grandmother..." he whispered. "She's all alone now. My aunt and cousin are gone. I don't want to study. Didi, I want to go home!"

Harsh could not bear to live away from home when his grandmother was in need. He had become so distressed about her that he was not able to focus on his studies at the Mercy Home. He appealed and received permission to return to his home in Nagpur. Undoubtedly, he has taken on the responsibilities of manhood and is doing his best. Perhaps someday Harsh will respond to Christ and not want to live his life without Him.

Philippians 1:23-25 - "But I am hard-pressed from both directions, having the desire to depart and be with Christ, for that is very much better; yet to remain on in the flesh is more necessary for your sake. Convinced of this, I know that I will remain and continue with you all for your progress and joy in the faith."

In the book of Philippians, Paul told the believers that he wanted to die and be with Christ but he knew that God wanted him to stay and teach the church for a little while longer. Sometimes, God may ask you to do something that you wish you did not have to do. If you love Jesus, you are always with the One who loves you most, even if you are separated from someone that you love. God will give you the strength to do His will.

CHAPTER 14

Without Him, I Am Nothing

"If you look at the world, you'll be distressed. If you look within, you'll be depressed If you look at God, you'll be at rest."

– Corrie Ten Boom

Sighing happily, Rani (pronounced "raw-knee") reverently turned the pages of her mother's Hindi Bible. A single candle flickered and cast shadows around the room. Her mother joined her on the cement floor and smiled expectantly. She didn't know how to read or write, so Rani read out loud to her every day. Pausing in first Corinthians, Rani ran her finger down the page to find their place. Stopping at chapter 13, she began to read.

"If I speak with the tongues of men and of angels, but do not have love, I have become a noisy gong or a clanging symbol. If I have the gift of prophecy, and know all mysteries, and all knowledge, and if I have all faith, so as to remove mountains, but do not have love, I am nothing. And if I give all my possessions to feed the poor, and if I surrender my body to be burned, but do not have love, it profits me nothing. Love is patient; love is kind and is not jealous. Love does not brag and is not arrogant, does not act unbecomingly; it does not seek its own, is not provoked, does not take into account a wrong suffered, does not rejoice in unrighteousness, but rejoices with the truth; bears all things, believes all things, hopes all things, endures all things..."

Rani remembered how lovingly her mother had treated her father after the horrible things he did to her. Guessing Rani's thoughts, her mother gave her a gentle hug.

"See, Rani, we just need to love your father and brother Rahul (pronounced "raw-hool"). They will see Jesus in us and maybe someday we'll get to read the Bible with them, too. It's time to sleep, dear; you have school in the morning."

Rani yawned and kissed her mother. She returned the Bible to its place in the corner of the room and crawled over to blow out the candle. As her eyes adjusted to the darkness, Rani laid down beside her brother Rahul. Rahul was only two years older than she, but he wasn't interested in staying up late to read the Bible or going to church on Sundays. Rani noticed that her mother had already fallen asleep in the other corner of the room.

"Love bears all things, believes all things, hopes all things, and endures all things." Rani repeated the words to herself and pictured her mother. In Rani's opinion, her mother had endured all things from her father. When Rani was six years old, her drunken father beat her mother with a knife until the woman became unconscious. Rickshaw drivers brought Rani's mother to the hospital where she was in a coma for two weeks. Rani and Rahul had stayed at the police station until their mother came out of her coma. Rani remembered how nervous she felt when her brother brought her home to be with their father again. Her mother assured her that her father would honor his promise to be gentle, but Rahul insisted their father was dangerous. Not two days later, Rani's father beat her mother again. That night, Rani and Rahul sneaked out of the house and boarded a train with their mother. They fled to Mumbai and lived with friends until Rani's mother found a room to rent.

Looking around the room, Rani thanked God for giving them this room. The third story apartment room wasn't like her home, but it was safe. Her mother paid for it by selling her blood every day to a blood bank. It wasn't wise to donate so much blood, but Rani's mother couldn't get another job and she had to pay the bills.

Although she suffered from severe physical weakness, Rani's mother leaned on the Lord for her strength. Rani drifted off to sleep praying that she would be as strong as her mother someday.

Several weeks later, Rani, Rahul and her mother went home to Nagpur to see their relatives. Rani had mixed feelings about the trip. She wanted to see her relatives and sometimes she wanted to see her father, but other times she felt nervous. Unexpectedly, her mother received a call from their landlord in Mumbai. Something was wrong with the apartment building and it was going to be torn down in two days. Rani's mother had to go back to Mumbai right away to find another apartment to rent. Wishing that Rani and Rahul would continue to study, Rani's grandmother offered to let them live with her and go to school. Rani and Rahul declined their grandmother's offer because they were naive to the potential danger, and still wanted to live with their father. Reluctantly, Rani's grandmother took them back to their old house to stay with him.

Several months later, Rani craned her neck to watch the sun set through the open front door. Brushing the sweat from her forehead, she finished sweeping the dirt floor. Putting the coconut frond broom away, the eleven year old went outside and gathered sticks from the brush and trash behind the house. When she returned to the house, Rani built a fire and cooked a handful of rice. Rahul joined her for dinner, but their father never came.

Rani washed the rice pot in the backyard and reentered the house. Even though they couldn't afford to buy candles, Rani had learned to see in the dark. She was thankful that their house only had one room so that it was easier to find her way around at night. As her eyes adjusted to the darkness, Rani recognized the form of her brother Rahul. He was so exhausted that he had fallen asleep leaning against the wall. She did not know when or if her father would come home, but she could wait. Her father habitually left home before the sun rose and did not return for hours or days at a time. He spent whatever he earned from his irregular job at the liquor store and came home drunk and irritable.

Rani felt like she hadn't slept for more than thirty minutes before she was rudely awakened by her father. His fists flew faster than his tongue as he ordered his children to get up and cook food for him. With a muffled cry, Rahul scrambled outside to collect brush for the fire. It took all Rani's strength to yank herself away from her father so she could fetch the rice. She pitied him as he staggered around the room muttering to himself and occasionally raising his voice to scold her. While the rice cooked, the delusional man continued to beat Rani and Rahul. He truly believed that they had not yet obeyed his command to feed him. Liquor was actively destroying him. After Rani's father ate his fill and fell asleep, she and Rahul dragged their injured bodies back into the corner and went back to sleep.

Rani's arms and legs ached from the new bruises, but she willed herself to ignore the pain and think about Jesus. How she wished she could read the Bible with her mother and hear her praying beside her again! "Love bears all things, believes all things, hopes all things, endures all things," she whispered. Picturing Jesus and His suffering, Rani resolved to wait patiently for God to take her back to a place where she was safe. She longed for the day that her father would understand God's love. Rani knew that without Christ, she was helpless. Her father did not know what he was doing because he did not know Christ. Rolling over, Rani whispered, "Because Jesus is with me, I can endure my father's beatings." Deep inside, she believed that Jesus would save her.

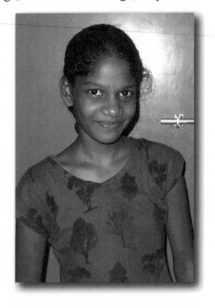

That summer, God answered Rani's prayers. A neighbor informed Rani's mother about the situation with her father and she came to visit. She heard about the Mercy Home and decided to take

Rani there. Rani was thrilled for the opportunity to go to church again. She had tried to go to school while she lived with her father, but she had become too exhausted and hungry to continue. At the Mercy Home, Rani could study, eat, and sleep in peace. She enjoys going on walks with the other girls her age and praying with them. Rani said, "I left my Bible with my mother in Mumbai, but here my friend Mariyam (pronounced "me-ree-um") is sharing hers with me. My brother Rahul met some Christian boys who brought him to church and now he knows Jesus. I am so happy that I can be here. Without God, I would not be here. I know what it feels like to be hurt, and I know that Jesus is the Healer. I want to become a doctor and tell hurting people about the One who loves them." Without Christ, Rani would not have survived, but in His care, she has everything she needs.

Psalm 66:8-12 - "Bless our God, O peoples, and sound His praise abroad, who keeps us in life, and does not allow our feet to slip. For you have tried us, O God, you have refined us as silver is refined. You brought us into the net; you laid an oppressive burden on our loins. You made men ride over our heads, we went through fire and through water, yet, you brought us out into a place of abundance."

No matter how hard your life may be, Jesus is always right there by your side. Struggles are opportunities to trust Him more. The next time you're crying or worrying about something, remember that God will take care of you and He can see the end result. With God's help, you can wait hopefully for what God will do.

Faith in God, good food and a safe life

CHAPTER 15

Shielded

"Faith does not know where it is being led, but it knows and loves the One who is leading."
                                    – Charles Spurgeon

Humidity wrapped the boys in a blanket of sweat as they pushed their way through the bamboo. Jivan (pronounced "jeev-on") tried to keep up with his companion and avoid snake holes. Green parrots cawed above their heads as the boys reached their favorite spot in the jungle. Jivan closed his eyes and lifted his hands towards the sky. Holding his breath, he thought of how Jesus was standing beside him. His friend Rupesh (pronounced "roo-pesh") dropped to his knees on the banana leaf mat they had made for their prayer spot.

"Lord Jesus," Jivan prayed, "we praise you for your creation and wisdom. As David said in the Psalms, You own the "cattle on a thousand hills" and you protect them day and night. Your presence is precious. Where two or three are gathered in your Name, you are there in their midst. Thank you for being with me and Rupesh in our special spot right now."

The boys prayed together for forty-five minutes before they rose to return to their duties at the government hostel. They had a strict schedule with a small amount of free time each day, and they chose to spend their free time talking to and about God. Rupesh's father, a Christian pastor, had given him a Bible that he treasured and shared with Jivan. Whenever the boys had a question about the Bible, they wrote it down and asked Rupesh's father about it later. Eagerly, Jivan had spent hours of his free time pouring over that Bible. Just like David and Jonathan did in the Bible, Rupesh and Jivan promised to pray for and with one another. Each week, as often as they had time, they would come to the jungle to pray where it was perfectly quiet.

"Rupesh," Jivan panted as they neared the hostel, "I'll miss you and our prayer times over summer vacation."

Rupesh looked sympathetic, then grinned. "I will miss praying with you too. But I know one thing you won't miss." His eyes twinkled with mischief.

"What?" Jivan paused, stubbing his right foot on a large root and catching his balance on a bamboo stalk.

"You won't miss trying to keep up with me! I can beat you in a race any day!" Rupesh laughed and bolted through the bamboo.

"Wait up!" Jivan called, checking for more tree roots before pursuing his friend.

Soon, Jivan and Rupesh were running back to the hostel to join the other 400-500 boys and girls for dinner. Jivan saw his older brother and sister in the hall. In one week, he knew that they would be going to their relative's house for the summer and everything would be completely different.

Jivan and his siblings painfully endured their time at their relatives' house. Their aunts and uncles had grown tired of caring for them over the years and decided to mistreat them to force them to leave. Jivan and his siblings were assigned certain difficult chores and told that if they did not complete the tasks, they would be beaten and not allowed to eat. Jivan often lay awake at night listening to his stomach growl and nursing his bruises. Finally, after six summers of abuse, his older brother Pitambar (pronounced "peat-ahm-bar") grew old enough to work and decided that Jivan and Meena had suffered enough. Despite the fact that the siblings were not very strong or experienced, they left their relatives and built a tiny hut of their own.

Pitambar became Jivan's father and protector. He earned seventy rupees (that is about one dollar and five cents in U.S. money) each day working as a construction worker. He used some of the money to buy food and the rest to send Jivan and Meena to the village school.

Although he was strict, Jivan appreciated Pitambar's leadership. He hoped that he would not have to think about his relatives or worry again.

Two years later, Jivan woke up one morning to the sound of his sister's voice. She was very upset about something. He could not roll over on his mat and ignore Meena even though the sun had not yet risen. As he came out of his sleep, he could heard the birds chirping outside their door, and realized that it was nearly time to get up and prepare for school.

"Jivan! Oh Jivan, come look, something awful has happened. I'm so afraid..." Meena choked down her sobs as Jivan stumbled to his feet and rubbed his eyes. Meena led him to Pitambar's bed and fell to her knees. Anxiously, Jivan grabbed his brother's wrist and searched for his pulse. His heart stopped. Pitambar was dead.

Stunned, Jivan spent two days grieving and contemplating the meaning of life. His name, Jivan, means "life" in Hindi, but after his brother died, Jivan did not feel like living. He and Meena had

heard that their uncle had killed him using witchcraft. Their father's brother was jealous of their twelve acre property and wanted to kill his brother's heirs in order to steal the land. How could his uncle hurt them like that? He thought that his brother might not be saved because the witchcraft had power over him. If only he could be with Pitambar one more time, to thank him for being father, mother, friend, and teacher to him. Jivan fell on his knees and wept before God. He knew that he was safe only because Jesus had placed a shield of protection around him. God showed him that life is short and he must choose to live his life for Christ.

Jivan's passion for Christ grew and he asked God to send him wherever He wanted him to serve. Jivan and his sister went to live at a Christian hostel that is run by the Indian Missionary Society. There, Jivan heard about Mission India Theological Seminary and believed that God prompted him to study theology in preparation for becoming a missionary in his hometown. Jivan continues to pray for others to come to Christ and receive the shield of protection that He provides.

1 Peter 2:9 - "But you are a chosen race, a royal priesthood, a holy nation, a people for God's own possession, so that you may proclaim the excellencies of Him who has called you out of darkness into his marvelous light."

The priests in the Bible were set apart to intercede for the people and to teach them about God. When God adopts you into His family, you can be sure that He will shield you and enable you to proclaim the truth to others.

CHAPTER 16
A Miracle In Me

"He is no fool who gives what he cannot keep to gain what he cannot lose."
– Jim Elliot, Missionary and Martyr in Ecuador

Ganesh (pronounced "gun-esh") shifted in his bamboo chair. A mosquito hummed in his ear. Annoyed, he half-heartedly batted the insect away. A single light bulb hung precariously from a cord on the roof of his snack stall. The stall was roughly eight feet long and five feet deep, a spacious room compared to most of the other booths that lined the street. The tin roof of the nearby railway station rattled as the wind lifted it up and down. Darkness wrapped the platform in a thick blanket, hiding the hundreds of orphans and beggars who slept near its tracks. No one seemed awake at 1am, but Ganesh was still afraid that someone might steal from him. Just then, a faint pair of headlights turned Ganesh's attention to the train tracks. A sleepy jeep driver steered the vehicle up onto the train tracks to avoid navigating the mud-caked roads. As the jeep rattled along the metal rails, the driver pressed the accelerator.

Strangely, Ganesh felt drawn to the tracks. For some reason, he decided to stretch his legs and walk towards the oncoming headlights. As he ambled along the train tracks, he saw countless figures strewn about the area. Children lined the tracks and trees, their rag-covered bodies exposed to the damp air. Most of them were orphans from the lower castes, but some had been abandoned by their relatives because of poverty. Deliberately, Ganesh turned away from the forlorn children and refocused on the vehicle approaching from the opposite direction. The jeep lights vaguely illuminated the tracks just long enough for Ganesh to spot something.

Ganesh wasn't the only one to notice something on the tracks. Squinting, the jeep driver concluded that it must be one of the wild animals that roamed the countryside. Nonchalantly, he continued to proceed without altering his course to avoid the creature. Ganesh continued from the opposite direction. Alarmed, he saw a tiny arm stretch out from the brown heap. He froze. It couldn't be true. It was a child.

Gripped with panic, Ganesh tried to scream, but the sound died in his throat. Every second, the jeep was coming closer to the child. Ganesh found his voice and shouted at the top of his lungs. Without warning, the jeep driver jerked the wheel to the left, narrowly missing the bundle on the tracks. Sweat streamed down Ganesh's face as he raced towards the child.

The driver stopped the jeep, apologizing and assuring Ganesh that he didn't know what the bundle was. He thanked the gods profusely because he believed that they had prevented him from killing the child. Just as quickly as he came, the driver left, leaving Ganesh to investigate.

Dropping to his knees, Ganesh examined the shabby brown rag that had hidden her body. She was just a toddler, and wore nothing but a filthy cloth tied around her waist. To his amazement, she was asleep. "It's a miracle she's alive. God must have a special plan for her," Ganesh breathed. Tenderly, he picked her up and cradled her in his arms. The malnourished girl shivered and Ganesh instinctively hugged her. He wondered why he suddenly felt compassion for this street child. She was no different than the hundreds of others who lived around the old platform. Every day, Ganesh saw scores of children begging, sleeping, and passing out at the railway platform. It was his job to ignore them so that they wouldn't disturb his shop. It was a miracle that he cared about her at all. Pulling the brown rag around her body, he paused to watch the toddler breathe.

Ganesh had to do something to protect this helpless, innocent child. He decided to bring her to his own home where she would be safe. His sister Sita (pronounced "sheet-uh") was a social worker; she would know just what to do for the child. His thoughts raced as he carefully closed up his shop, frequently checking to make sure he didn't wake the feather-weight child resting on his shoulder. As the sun rose over the railroad platform, Ganesh carried his new treasure home.

Ganesh's sister Sita spent days questioning the villagers about the child's family while the toddler stayed home with her elderly father. Eventually, Sita found the little girl's father and learned the horrible truth about what had happened to Khushbu (pronounced "koosh-boo"). Her father, a hopeless alcoholic, had married another woman with a son after Khushbu's mother had died. His new wife did not want Khushbu, and left her at the railroad station, hoping that the toddler would not be able to find her way back home. Enraged at this atrocity, Sita vowed to confront Khushbu's father about his responsibility for the inhumane treatment of his daughter. Tragically, she found the drunk man on his deathbed. He died after he begged Sita to swear to take care of Khushbu. True to her word, Sita legally adopted Khushbu and homeschooled her for one year. She would have kept Khushbu longer, but the neighbors heard Khushbu's story and made multiple attempts to kidnap her and sell her into slavery. She was a potentially easy target because Sita's elderly father could not adequately protect her in their home. Ganesh advised Sita to send Khushbu to live in a small government-run hostel where she would be safe. Reluctantly, Sita took Khushbu to a hostel some distance away from their village and promised to keep in touch with her.

Although Khushbu enjoyed her studies at the government hostel, she missed Sita and her spicy curry. Since there were only twenty children at the hostel, they all sat in a circle and ate together on the kitchen floor. The staff did their best to care for the children and send them all to school, but they had limited money and the food was minimal. Khushbu excelled in her studies and relished every opportunity she had to learn something new. Whenever the hostel had visitors or special meetings in the community, Khushbu was asked to speak. One of her speeches was printed in the newspaper. Even though she was quite talented, Khushbu felt like she was missing something. What if there was something more to life that she had not yet found? Somehow, the now twelve year old girl felt that she needed to go somewhere new to find the answers to her questions.

Insisting that there was something she was missing, Khushbu expressed her desire to leave the government hostel the next time she talked with Sita on the phone. Meanwhile, Sita's Christian cousin had visited Sita and advised her to send Khushbu to Mission India's Mercy Home. When Sita and Khushbu discussed the recommendation, they decided to see if the Christians could help answer her questions about life. A short time later, Sita took Khushbu to the Mercy Home. Since she was already used to hostel life, it did not take

her very long to adjust. Within one week of her arrival, she had begun to explore Christianity. As she eagerly read the Bible, Jesus revealed Himself to her as her Savior and Lord. Grateful for the amazing forgiveness of God for all her sins, she joyfully opened her heart to Christ. Although Sita did not believe that Jesus was the only God, she respected Khushbu's decision and began to call her for advice and prayer.

"Yes Sita, I have been praying for you. I will fast for three days about this. Don't worry, the Lord will provide a good husband for you," Khushbu assured Sita over the phone. Someone had just asked her father for her hand in marriage and she wanted Khushbu to pray for her. Sita believed in many gods, and thought that perhaps Jesus was one of the more powerful ones. Having previously declined a proposal from a man who refused to adopt Khushbu, she hesitated before she replied.

"I want to believe that you're right. You know that I promised the gods that I would not marry any man unless he were willing to accept you as my daughter. I don't know if there is such a man, but you are my greatest treasure. Thank you for fasting for me, Khushbu. I will call you as soon as the men make a decision." Khushbu marveled that Sita, a Hindu social worker, would love her so much.

God has filled Khushbu's life with miracles. Amazingly, He has spared her life and brought her to the Mercy Home where she heard the gospel. There, God surrounded her with people who loved her. Although Sita and her brother Ganesh are Hindu, they recognize that a powerful God is in Khushbu's life. They did not scold her when she professed faith and was baptized in 2012. God has given Sita a loving husband and has blessed Khushbu with an adoptive father who loves her dearly and calls her frequently. Khushbu is now seventeen and working on her second year of college. Her goal is to become a nurse and point people to the God of miracles.

Colossians 1:13-14 - "For He rescued us from the domain of darkness, and transferred us to the kingdom of His beloved Son, in whom we have redemption, the forgiveness of sins."

The Lord can rescue anyone and He wants to transfer people from darkness to light by adopting them into His family. Sin is anything that you think, say, or do that breaks God's law of perfect love. We cannot help but sin every day, and because God is perfect, He cannot have sin in His presence in heaven. The punishment for our sin is eternal separation from God. In order to make a way for us to be with Him, God chose to pour out the punishment we deserve onto Jesus when He died on the cross. Jesus loved us so much that He was willing to take our punishment for sin and give us His perfect righteousness. Some people think that if they are really good, God will let them into heaven, but the Bible does not say that. The Bible says that if you admit that you have sinned, believe what the Bible says about what Jesus did, and accept God's gift of the righteousness of Jesus, then God will adopt you into his family. Isn't that a miracle? Because of Jesus, we can enjoy the blessings of being in God's family now and also forever in heaven. How wonderful it will be to see the Lord who has been our Shepherd and Provider and to worship him with all the Christians from every country, language, and century! Together, we will praise Him forever and ever.

About Saji Lukos

Dr. Saji Lukos is the Founder of Reaching Indians Ministries International (RIMI—USA), and Mission India (MI—India). His educational background includes a Master's degree in business, a Master of Divinity (Missions) from Trinity International University in Deerfield IL, and a Doctorate in Ministry from Bethel University in St. Paul MN.

Today RIMI/MI has become a major mission in India reaching people in every state of India with the message of Christ through three programs-Evangelism and Church Planting, Leadership and Compassion. Over 1500 missionaries are serving with Mission India. In addition to it, there a major seminary Nagpur (www.mits-india.org) and 29 Bible schools. Saji's passion is to raise up 100,000 Christ-like leaders within the next twenty years. Thus he is intentionally raising up 1000 pastors/leaders who will develop 100 leaders within the next 10-20 years.

Saji and Mony live in Round Lake Beach, IL, USA. They have a grown-up daughter Maryann, who is a school teacher in Waukegan.

Also by Saji Lukos

Transformed for a Purpose

Transformed for a Purpose is a compelling dramatic narrative of how God rescued a man and his family from the bondage of Satan to impact a nation with the Gospel of Jesus Christ.

Dr. Lukos writes with passion from an experience with Christ that overflows through the book. His story will both inspire and challenge the reader to greater resolve to seek first the Kingdom.

The One True God

The One True God is a masterful compilation of compelling stories how the One True God intervened in the lives of desperate men and women.

In this book, Saji with help of his associate writer Susan Lester, shares how lives that were once filled with revenge and murder are profoundly changed into a life filled with love and mercy. From death to life; from sickness to health; each story is unique and proof of the miraculous love of the One True God.

Kingdom Leadership

Kingdom Leadership is a must read book for any leader who wants to make a transformational and lasting impact in the world. The Kingdom principles Dr. Lukos used to build his ministry were learned and implemented during 25 years of pioneering experience in the ministry of RIMI and Mission India. *Kingdom Leadership* will inspire and challenge you to pursue the Kingdom path for your ministry as Saji boldly shares his painful yet purposeful life experiences around a Kingdom perspective. The twelve leadership principles in this book are not only based on authentic personal lessons but are duplicable if you have a passion to change the world.

*For more information about RIMI
and to find out about other materials
available, please visit*

www.RIMI.org

You can also contact us at:

RIMI
1949 Old Elm Road
Lindenhurst, IL 60046, USA
847.265.0630
info@rimi.org

Hope In The Darkness
Order Form

I would like to help the ministry by sponsoring:

❒ **Child**   ❒ **Missionary:** ❒ $30 ❒ $60 ❒ $120

❒ **Bicycle** $100 ❒ **Motorbike** $1,500

❒ **Where Most Needed** $_____

Please send me ____ more books at $16.95 + $4.50 Ship/Hndl each

for a total of $_____ (Call for quantity shipping rates)

Total Funds Enclosed $_____

_____
Name

_____
Address

_____
Address

_____
City / State / Zip Code

_____
Phone

_____
Praises and Prayers

_____
Email

Credit Card: ❒ Visa ❒ MasterCard ❒ American Express ❒ Discover

Name as it appears on Card

_____ _____ _____
Number   Expiration Date   Total

_____
Signature

RIMI
1949 Old Elm Road, Lindenhurst, IL 60046
Phone: 847.265.0630 Fax: 847.265.0642
Email: ministry@RIMI.org Web: www.RIMI.org

Please make checks payable to RIMI
RIMI is a 501(c)(3) organization and
all donations, except for books are tax
deductable. A receipt will be sent
for those items that qualify.

RIMI REACHING INDIANS MINISTRIES INTERNATIONAL

ECFA MEMBER

Hope In The Darkness
Order Form

I would like to help the ministry by sponsoring:

❐ **Child**   ❐ **Missionary:** ❐ $30 ❐ $60 ❐ $120

❐ **Bicycle** $100 ❐ **Motorbike** $1,500

❐ **Where Most Needed** $_____

Please send me _____ more books at $16.95 + $4.50 Ship/Hndl each

for a total of $_____ (Call for quantity shipping rates)

Total Funds Enclosed $_____

_____
Name

_____
Address

_____
Address

_____
City / State / Zip Code

_____
Phone

_____
Praises and Prayers

_____
Email

Credit Card: ❐ Visa   ❐ MasterCard   ❐ American Express   ❐ Discover

Name as it appears on Card

_____   _____ _____
Number   Expiration Date   Total

_____
Signature

<table>
<tr><td>RIMI
1949 Old Elm Road, Lindenhurst, IL 60046
Phone: 847.265.0630 Fax: 847.265.0642
Email: ministry@RIMI.org Web: www.RIMI.org</td><td>Please make checks payable to RIMI
RIMI is a 501(c)(3) organization and all donations, except for books are tax deductable. A receipt will be sent for those items that qualify.</td></tr>
</table>

REACHING INDIANS
MINISTRIES INTERNATIONAL

Please cut along dotted line